The Cassandra Effect

The Cassandra Effect
Future Perceptions on Air Power

Sanu Kainikara

Vij Books India Pvt Ltd
New Delhi (India)

Copyright © 2016, *Sanu Kainikara*

Dr Sanu Kainikara
416, The Ambassador Apartments
2 Grose Street
Deakin, ACT 2600, Australia
sanu.kainikara@gmail.com

First Published in 2016

ISBN : 9789385563324 (Paperback)

ISBN : 978-93-85563-82-9 (ebook)

Designed and Setting by

Vij Books India Pvt Ltd
2/19, Ansari Road, Darya Ganj, New Delhi - 110002, India
(www.vijbooks.com)

All rights reserved.

No part of this book may be reproduced, stored in a retrieval system, transmitted or utilized in any form or by any means, electronic, mechanical, photocopying, recording or otherwise, without the prior permission of the copyright owner. Application for such permission should be addressed to the author.

Dedicated to all Air Warriors
Whose implicit belief in flight
Has made possible the improbable...
Touching the sky with glory!

BOOKS BY THE SAME AUTHOR

Papers on Air Power

Pathways to Victory

Red Air: Politics in Russian Air Power

Australian Security in the Asian Century

A Fresh Look at Air Power Doctrine

Friends in High Places

Seven Perennial Challenges to Air Forces

The Art of Air Power: Sun Tzu Revisited

At the Critical Juncture

Essays on Air Power

The Bolt from the Blue

The Asian Crucible

Political Musings: Turmoil in the Middle-East

The Indian History Series: From Indus to Independence

Volume I: Prehistory to the Fall of the Mauryas

Volume II: The Classical Age

Volume III: The Disintegration of Empires

Cassandra

Cassandra, also known as Alexandra or Kassandra, was the daughter of King Priam and Queen Hecuba of Troy.

In Greek mythology it is commonly believed that Cassandra was given the power of prophesy by Apollo in order to seduce her. However, when she refused he 'spat' in her mouth cursing her never to be believed. This curse manifested in Cassandra being considered insane, although it is also mentioned that she was merely misunderstood.

Cassandra is an enduring archetype and a modern invocation of the paradox—the ability to predict the future accurately but not being believed, an inconsistency under which most air power strategists have laboured over the past century—results in the main title of this monograph: The Cassandra Effect.

'Developers and demonstrators of new technology typically encounter scepticism or derision, and in aeronautics it was ever thus.'

Richard P. Hallion[1]

---

1 Hallion, Richard P., 'Air and Space Power: Climbing and Accelerating', in Olsen, John Andreas (ed), *A History of Air Warfare*, Potomac Books Inc., Washington, D.C., 2010, p. 371.

Contents

Author's Preface		xi
Introduction		xix
Chapters		1
1.	Air Power and the Evolving Character of War	1
2.	Politics and Air Power	19
3.	The Challenge of Cutting-Edge Technology	35
4.	Air Power Systems—Inhabited, Uninhabited and Autonomous	57
5.	Air Force: Future Focal Points	75
Conclusion		87
Selected Bibliography		93
Index		95

AUTHOR'S PREFACE

'Men, my brothers, men the workers, ever reaping
something new;
That which they have done but earnest of the things
that they shall do;
For I dipt into the future, far as human eye could see,
Saw the Vision of the world, and all the wonder that
would be;
Saw the heavens fill with commerce, argosies of
magic sails,
Pilots of the purple twilight, dropping down with
costly bales;
Heard the heavens fill with shouting, and there rain'd
a ghastly dew
From the nations' airy navies grappling in the central
blue.'

Lord Alfred Tennyson,

Locksley Hall, 1842

I have been a lifelong and passionate advocate of air power. Obviously this comes from my choice of a profession and the opportunities that it provided me to have a grandstand view of what air power could accomplish when employed by professional masters. Further, my gradual evolution from being at the tip of the spear to developing an understanding of air power within the broader military power and national security equation has made me have an increased respect and understanding for the application of air power as an element of national power. However, the very same development has also inculcated a deep-seated pragmatism in all my analysis regarding its capabilities.

I have been one to clearly mention the limitations of air power, particularly in its application within stringent rules of engagements and the challenges that it invariably faces when employed as a force projection capability. At the same time I have also noticed a trend in recent times to dismiss the criticality of air power to the optimised employment of military power, especially by arm-chair strategists who are projected by the media as being experts. The fall-out of such ill-informed discussions has been that the independent status of air forces—the normal repository of a nation's air power capabilities—is itself being questions as being superfluous to a nation's security needs. The tangential path of this logic makes me question the veracity of the thinking process of the people who advocate the abolishing of independent air forces. I honestly believe that these, somewhat heretical, ideas have the capacity to be fancied by less than well-informed strategic decision-makers as resource-saving measures. If such a concept takes hold within the national ethos and is acted upon, that particular nation will have forfeited its ability to protect its sovereignty. In a truly democratic nation popular perception is everything when it comes to understanding its security challenges. Therefore, the means to successfully address these challenges and ensure that national security imperatives are met will also have to take into account the perception of the people. In other words, the debate regarding the crucial part that air power plays in ensuring national security cannot be left to broad and biased debates.

Here I must mention a book published in 2011 by the revered military historian and air power analyst, Martin van Creveld, called *The Age of Air Power*.[1] The book takes the overall view that although air power was indeed very effective, and at times even critical to the success of military operations in a number of conflicts of the past, its helicon days are over and that it is currently in terminal decline. While Professor Creveld does provide some broad reasoning for his assertion, I found that almost all his arguments against air power could also be very easily put forward coherently as points that indicate the continuing rise of air power as a primary element of national power. Further, the final chapter of the book, *'Going Down, 1945 - ?'* does not provide any conclusive evidence to nail down the central argument and hypothesis

---

1 Creveld, Martin van, *The Age of Air Power*, Public Affairs, New York, 2011.

of the book—that air power had outlived its usefulness and become redundant as an instrument of power projection. It is paradoxical that almost at the same time that this renowned professor was denigrating air power, NATO was intervening rather successfully in Libya under the aegis of the United Nations, almost exclusively through use of air power. In one fell sweep Operation Unified Protector completely negated the doomsday predictions regarding the demise of air power that had been put forward in the book under discussion.

The continuing success of the employment of air power in the succeeding five years since 2011, when the book was published, has only reasserted my belief that air power is a foundational requirement to build the edifice of national security. I am convinced that this belief will stand the onslaught of disparate challenges. From its very inception more than a century ago as an instrument of military power, visionary thinkers had predicted that the future of military power will always have to embrace the all-encompassing nature of air power. This was despite the naysayers who dismissed the fledgling capability as nothing more than a passing fancy. The thinking seems to have come full circle now, in the early decades of the 21st century. This is indeed surprising since the world is poised to leap into the technological unknown. The views expressed in this monograph has been percolating in my mind ever since I read the negative arguments in *The Age of Air Power*. However, I hasten to add that this book is not meant as a rebuttal to the much acclaimed and internationally recognised author of the book. The contents of this book are my personal views and opinions regarding future trends in the development and employment of air power. The predictions may seem far-fetched at times, but then who has seen the future with any assurance of certainty? Having said that, and totally aware of our limited ability to predict the future with any assured accuracy, I am willing to 'stick my head out' and say that the age of air power is only beginning, not coming to an end.

There is a prevailing belief that history, or the past, is highly unlikely to repeat itself. This may indeed be so. However, anyone who dabbles in predicting the future should also be aware of the caveat that the present and even the future will invariably rhyme with the past. This becomes more than amply apparent when historical events are analysed or considered in the broadest possible terms. However, the adage cannot be applied in its simplistic form to the employment of air power, or for that matter power projection through the employment of any element of national power. Of course, there is no doubt that the fundamentals that guide the application of air power—essentially its guiding philosophical doctrine—will by and large remain unchanged except for minor adaptations. However, the actual employment of air power through the myriad assets and systems that generate, apply and sustain it will be a constantly changing equation. This must be so, especially since the adversaries who face the full brunt of air power are equally adept at countering and neutralising air power's inherent asymmetry. Future concepts and operational application of air power are not likely to rhyme very well with the past—unfortunately.

Even as air power's considerable power projection capabilities are being inexorably improved, it also faces many challenges, some major and some of a minor nature. These challenges in isolation or in combination have the capacity to shake the belief in the ability of air power to transcend increasing difficulties that seem to erupt in the battlespace. However, such situations will be few and far in between. In the ever changing global security scenario, it is certain that air power will be called upon to undertake even more crucial roles to ensure national security. Almost like the proverbial vicious cycle, this increased responsibility will be accompanied by unexpected challenges that will have to be correctly anticipated, accurately analysed and comprehensively addressed. This is the bane of any capability that functions at the cutting edge of technology and employs continually evolving concepts of operations: air power is no exception, and is perhaps the best example.

On the other hand, the greatly enhanced operational efficiency that air power demonstrates has transformed the manner in which it is viewed at the strategic level of national security decision-making. Although military intervention, even in places far away from the homeland, continues to be pursued as a requirement to ensure national security and to protect national interests, there is a marked reluctance on the part of the democratic and more developed world to commit land forces to combat as part of such interventions. In combination with this demonstrated reluctance to put land forces in harm's way, air power's ability to be precise, discriminate and proportional in the application of lethal force has made it the first-choice option for nations with capable air forces. This trend will only be reinforced into the future.

In this monograph I have intentionally not analysed cyberspace, which although considered a separate domain, is difficult to define. Today there is a great deal of debate regarding who owns cyberspace, with a number of air forces staking their claims to its ownership. I believe that the cyber domain cannot be owned by an individual Service; it will not be a viable approach. The impracticality of such an attempt is especially manifest in small air forces and middle-powers. Cyberspace has to be viewed as a national capability with its exploitation and defence being dealt with at a level above that of the pure military strategic one. However, since air power, more than any other military capability, is completely dependent on cyberspace for its efficient and effective application, air forces must contribute directly to its defence within a whole-of-nation approach to cyber security. Cyberspace and activities within the domain, however it is defined, are still evolving and needs to be carefully monitored.

Successful air forces, the primary repository of air power in most nations, are always 'learning organisations' that can collectively look at the past, analyse the present and produce a credible road map for the future. The success of an air force is built on the personnel being able to exploit every opportunity that presents itself to ensure that the much vaunted flexibility, agility and adaptability of air power is always maintained at an optimal state to be employed. If this cannot be ensured, there is a high probability of the air force becoming irrelevant at the strategic level of national security and being gradually swept aside. However, the hard fact is that a nation without a credible air force can never assume the sanctity of its sovereignty. It is incumbent on the men and women who advocate air power to ensure that the nation's air force does not ever falter.

There is a caveat that I must mention at the very beginning of this monograph. The statements and ideas mentioned in the chapters that constitute the book have not been provided with any references. This is solely because they have been arrived at over a number of years of reading, thinking and speculating and cannot be attributed to anything but my own personal thought process. Yes, there will be similarities and impetus to how a particular idea has germinated, but

I can state with clarity that the growth of a particular notion has been a process that I have undertaken on my own. Therefore, if some of those concepts and ideas sound a bit 'off', I alone carry the blame. They cannot be attributed to anyone else! The lack of references is therefore, deliberate.

Let me finish by sharing three of my cardinal 'beliefs' regarding the future of air power. First, air power is critical to the effectiveness of any military force and the success of its operations. It will continue to increase in importance as a war-winning element, even when faced with adversaries who do not have any significant air power capabilities. Second, air power will continue to dominate the battlespace with its enhanced ability to strike precisely at time-critical targets, a focused requirement for military forces that is gradually becoming the norm. A combination of air power's inherent ISR and precision strike capabilities make air power omnipotent in the contemporary battlespace. Third, all nations that have a robust national security strategy will continue to nurture a calculated minimum level of air power capabilities. This is so even while the acrimonious debate regarding expenditure involved with the acquisition, maintenance and sustainment of air power capabilities will continue to percolate, especially in democratic nations.

I believe that demonstrated all-round air power capability will be 'the' deterrent factor well into the future. A capable air force and a demonstrated national will to employ it to ensure national sovereignty will be at the vanguard of security strategies. This combination will always make potential adversaries think twice before initiating any action that is inimical to the security interests of the nation. The bottom line however is that such a credible capability comes at a price! A nation will have to accept the expenses of maintaining a credible air force as the premium to be paid for the insurance of national security.

Sanu Kainikara

Canberra

August 2016

Not to have an adequate air force in the present state of the world is to compromise the foundations of national freedom and independence.

> Winston Churchill, *House of Commons, 14 March 1933*.

… then there was war in heaven. But it was not angels. It was that small golden zeppelin, like a long oval world, high up. It seemed as if the cosmic order were gone, as if there had come a new order, a new heavens above us: and as if the world in anger were trying to revoke it … So it seems our cosmos is burst, burst at last, the stars and Moon blown away, the envelope of the sky burst out, and a new cosmos appeared, with a long-ovate, gleaming central luminary, calm and drifting in a glow of light, like a new Moon, with its light bursting in flashes on the earth, to burst away the earth also. So it is the end — our world is gone, and we are like dust in the air.

> Milton, *Paradise Lost*.

INTRODUCTION

'For the first time in some 5,000 years of military history—5,000 years of history of man taking organised forces into combat—we saw an independent air operation produce a political result. What that means for the future we will still have to divine... This kind of utility can do nothing but place greater demands on air and space forces for the future.'

General Mike Dugan, USAF Retired

Commenting on *Operation Allied Force* in Kosovo, 1999

The volatility of the international security environment makes it impossible to predict the future with any level of credible assurance. In these circumstances the only surety is that all nations who can afford it will maintain military forces with as much capability as can be mustered within the resource constraints of the nation. However, a credible military force has to be balanced, which is a triumvirate consisting of land, naval and air forces. So it is not difficult to conclude that air forces—and by extension air power—will continue to be part of the national security calculus well into the foreseeable future.

From its inception as a war-fighting capability, air power has faced numerous challenges to its development and employment—from the tactical and operational levels of its application to the strategic level where it connects with national security requirements. It is not an exaggeration to state that the very need to have an independent air force has been, and at times even now continues to be, questioned. The debate regarding the independent status of air forces can, with absolute conviction, be discarded as the brainchild of extremely parochial, biased and less than well-informed individuals. Those who would continue to argue, in the 21st century that an independent air force nested within the broader military capabilities of a nation is not needed to ensure national security cannot be considered sufficiently knowledgeable regarding the challenges to national sovereignty and protecting national interests. They should not be taken seriously.

Air power has been a military capability for just over a century. Therefore, what is most striking about air power and its rapid development is the ease with which it has claimed centre-stage status in the triumvirate of military powers. (Here military capabilities resident in the space and cyber domains have been discounted, since they span all three traditional domains and are of relatively recent origin in comparison to air power.) How did air power become such a critical element within the power projection capabilities of a nation? And, why is it now being considered the first-choice response option when there is a perceived need to employ force in the pursuit of national security imperatives?

The answers to both the questions are not straightforward and any explanation will have to take into consideration the contemporary interconnected world and the currently-in-vogue, nuanced interpretation of the concept of national security. A simple and basic truth, which no one debates or doubts, is the fact that all military capabilities have to be oriented towards achieving the requirements of national security. Air forces and their resident air power capabilities are no exceptions. However, when the fundamental concept of national security is not static but an evolving entity, it creates a direct and cascading effect on the military capability development processes, at times creating a dissonance that is detrimental. This statement needs elaboration. One of the primary considerations to capability development is the possible manner in which the future force will be employed and the effects that it will be required to create. In turn, this will be influenced by the security perceptions and threat assessments of the nation, which in themselves are not static, but influenced by a number of other factors. The nuanced nature of national security is the result. From this grows the necessity to design a capability development process that can keep pace with the changing demands of national security.

The current global security environment is such that almost all perceivable threats to national security are amorphous and may not be aimed directly at any one nation. The volatile Middle-East Asia remains an exception to this generality. The democratic world is facing threats fundamentally aimed at creating overarching changes to the existing value system of the world at large. In the long-term the greatest threats to the democratic world are those aimed at altering the current concepts of nation-states, while targeting individual liberty and collective freedom. In such an all-encompassing scenario, the security challenges facing democratic nations are immense and complex. Of necessity, the military forces are at the forefront of facing the challenge, shouldering an onerous responsibility.

It is equally important to understand that the prevailing threat scenario is not one that can be labelled purely a military threat, it covers a far broader security envelope. It is obvious then that the emerging challenges cannot be countered and fully defeated by a military force alone, irrespective of its capability and capacity to inflict lethal damage and/or create effects. The response to emerging national threats will have to come from an optimum combination of all elements of national power, of which the military forms but one component, albeit a critical one. The response to contemporary threats would have to be aimed at the cognitive domain of the adversary rather that at the physical level. The physical actions should remain only a peripheral and carefully tailored response to contain the environment. The success or failure of the security response will depend on the ability of a nation to balance these two somewhat separate initiatives. The suggestion here is that the response has to be holistic and balanced, which can only be created successfully by a studied whole-of-government approach to national security.

The Quandary of Predicting the Future

Crystal gazing is often an interesting pastime. It can be said that it is at best an extremely difficult exercise and at worst a completely foolhardy enterprise. On a more even keel judgement, it becomes an issue only when the pronouncements have to be corroborated with logical forward reasoning based on facts that can be ascertained here and now. Narrowing down future predictions to the ones that pertain to national security is perhaps even more difficult, especially since the international order is in a constant state of flux. The probability of a prediction coming true reduces dramatically in such situations. In these circumstances, when there is no assured way to predict the future, it can be said that the future will always remain full of questions with no clear answers. This might indeed be true.

There is a however a method that, if properly employed, could make dealing with this complexity a bit easier. The future could become a little less opaque if the past and the present are studied and the thread that links the progression of events from the past to the present carefully identified. While this process seems easy and straight forward, it is not so. Identifying the common thread that traverses the past into the present is difficult because it is not always easy to find the cause and effect in a continuous manner even when the events of the past are clearly visible. However, detailed reflection on visible developmental trends from the immediate and medium term past makes it easier to identify the continuity. Once the thread has been identified it can be extrapolated into the future to gain a fairly reliable and coherent view of what the future might hold, at least in the near-term. The reliability of this process increases with the increase in the influence of individual events of the past being examined. The probability of accuracy of a prediction is highest when there is technical clarity and focus with the unknown being only a relatively small percentage of the whole.

Future National Security

The world is going through one of the most strategically confronting eras in modern history. The times are troubled and military forces the world over are faced with complex challenges—in their operational employment, in developing a force structure that will adequately cater for the greatly expanded spectrum of operations, and in ensuring that they are capable of creating the desired effects at the time and place required. Planning therefore becomes a foundational requirement for the success of a military force in all its employment; whether in benign humanitarian aid and disaster relief (HADR) or in the lethal application of force at the highest end of the operational spectrum. The baseline requirement is to ensure adequacy of response.

So what will the future concept of national security be like? First, there is one broad strategic level factor that can be assumed with a great deal of assurance for the future—large-scale, state-on-state wars conducted

Introduction

by state-owned conventional military forces are highly unlikely to take place in the near or mid-term future. However, this does not mean that conventional military forces have suddenly become redundant. Quite the contrary. In fact the destructive power resident in modern military forces is a dominant factor that acts as a primary deterrent to states initiating military actions that would lead to such a conflict. It can be safely assumed that conventional military forces are unlikely to be employed in the future in traditional military versus military confrontations.

If this assumption that traditional employment is unlikely is true, the obvious question that comes up is regarding their viability and contribution to national security. It is certain that no government will willingly expend the huge resource outlay necessary to raise, train and sustain a modern military force if they do not contribute directly and visibly to national security. In this context, the concept of national security needs to be understood in a very broad manner, ensuring that it spans activities ranging from relatively benign ones initiated to influence and shape the environment to the other end of the spectrum where a war of national survival itself may have to be fought. Military forces are increasingly being employed throughout this spectrum to enhance national security.

In the past few decades a visible trend has become noticeable in the national security calculus. Governments around the world are becoming increasingly reliant on military forces to bring succour to people affected by natural disasters and/or man-made catastrophes and to stabilise the more volatile regions, both domestically and internationally. This could be the result of nations not having recourse to any other equally well organised body capable of responding as rapidly and cohesively as the military forces. The broadening of the concept of national security has automatically expanded the spectrum of operations of traditional military forces.

Within this expanded spectrum, force projection is the most critical undertaking of military forces. It is therefore incumbent on decision-makers to understand the directional thrust of force projection capability development and to view this process through the prism of national security imperatives. Only this combined but dual activity will ensure that both are in consonance with each other, as far as possible. Ideally they should be fully and completely aligned, but extraneous factors such as resource availability could create a slight and nuanced variation between the two. Such variations must be carefully managed so that there is no visible disharmony, which could rapidly form a schism in times of national stress. Failure to do so could have disastrous consequences for national security.

Air Power

A competent military force will have an independent air force as part of its fundamental capability equation. This is so because the air domain envelopes the other two physical domains and functions as a controlling element in almost all operations. Since military forces can be termed the final arbiters in the sphere of national security and air power is a critical element of military power, it is incumbent on air power practitioners to be cognisant of three strategic factors: they must be aware of the constantly altering outlines of the envelope of national security; they must keep a constant monitoring watch on the latest developments taking place in air power technology, its application, concepts of operations and overarching strategic imperatives; and they must be able to combine a clear understanding of air power and national security to look as far ahead as possible into the future.

There are increasing challenges to the employment of air power in the lethal strike role and more broadly in contributing to the current conflict environment of irregular wars, which tend to make military forces focus on a very small section of the larger spectrum of conflict. The strategic relevance of air power within the national security apparatus is directly dependent on its ability to provide the national leadership with tangible and multiple options to ameliorate emerging security challenges, across the entire spectrum of conflict. This requires air power strategists to be able to offer the appropriate suite of air power capabilities to cater for the current conflict while continuing to maintain its strategic capabilities at readiness for emerging eventualities. This is a complex and elaborate exercise that involves astute allocation of resources, fine tuning of training and education, and aligning capability development with anticipated future needs. The long lead-time required to create and deploy air power capabilities further complicates this process.

Since air power has been at the forefront of IW for more than a decade, there is a natural tendency to structure the entire force for irregular conflicts and asymmetric application. If such an approach is taken it would mean that air power is actively preparing for the last fight than looking ahead to emerging challenges of the future. While predicting the future is never an easy task, it is incumbent on air power practitioners to clear the cobwebs that shroud the future and be cognisant of evolving security threats that will have to be overcome. All conflicts—conventional and irregular—require the concerted application of air power to ensure victory. This is an irrefutable fact. The core competencies of air power should be enhanced while retaining the basic adaptability in order to ensure that no surprise sprung in the future becomes insurmountable. Air power should continue to be able to produce the necessary effects, when and where required. The future relevance of air power as an element of national power will depend entirely on this one factor.

The question is what will future air power look like—in terms of the capabilities that it will bring to bear to create the desired effects; the systems that will deliver these capabilities; and the concepts of operations that will facilitate their optimum employment. The answers to these vexed questions cannot be easily conjured up, and even after deep analysis the answers that emerge will only be, at best, partially correct. However, by extending the line of development of capabilities and concepts forward in the same trajectory as they have been in the past few decades, it will be possible to arrive at some believable answers. This book is an attempt at doing so.

Future Relevance

If there is a factor that can be singled out as being critical to the future relevance of an air force, it would have to be the professional mastery of the force. If this can be ensured, it will not be wrong to state that in a very broad manner the advantages that air power brings to the military forces of a nation and its direct contribution to national security will not diminish into the future. In fact, with the increasing efficiency in its application, its importance will also increase. The fundamental idea of projecting power from the third dimension is here to stay—evolution will take place in the systems that are fielded and the concepts within which they are employed. Similarly the fundamental roles that air power delivers—control of the air, strike, air mobility, and ISR—will also be enduring. Changes will take place only in the manner in which they are achieved. The future relevance of air power as an element of national power can never be questioned, provided professional mastery of air power, individual and collective, can be assured.

Does this mean that a broad brush template can be created for the future application of air power? The answer would have to be an unequivocal no. It is only possible to glean the possible future employment of air power from the air campaigns that have been conducted in the near past and the ones that are on-going at the moment. The surety is that air power will be repeatedly used as an element of national power to demonstrate a nation's will and determination to act decisively, in pursuance of varied national interests. Air power has the advantage of being able to accomplish this in places far away from the home country very fast and also to establish the credibility of the nation as a responsible international citizen through the rapid provision of humanitarian aid and disaster relief in times of need. Irrespective of the myriad nay-sayers peddling their warped view of air power, this is the reality in the modern world that reality will also stand the test of time.

Nations that aspire to influence the geo-political landscape positively, will per force have to maintain robust air power capabilities that can be innovatively employed across the entire spectrum of conflict and can contribute in the broadest sense possible to national security. Future concepts of operations and capability acquisition will, or ideally should, always reflect this fundamental paradigm.

The Cassandra Effect

War has always been a part of human history and continues to be part of the global political process, irrespective of attempts to minimise the probability of it breaking out. The fact is that wars and conflicts—actual or threatened—are an indelible part of the negotiating process between sovereign states. While the nature of war remains conclusively embedded in the political process, its characteristics and conduct have altered over the years. They continue to evolve, almost as a constant process. These changes are influenced by technological innovations, the context of the conflict and the ethos of the participants.

This monograph is an attempt at examining the major trends that are likely to be noticeable in the development of air power in the future. It does not claim to be exhaustive in its research, nor does it claim to be accurate to the n-th degree in its predictions. The author has put his considerable experience in the practical application as well as the study of air power into the creation of this document. While there is a selected bibliography at the end of the book, the use of footnotes have been resorted to only very restrictively. The reason primarily is that a number of conclusions have been arrived at based on practical experience and the individual thought process of the author. Therefore, the reader is at liberty to discount all or any of them.

Chapter 1 examines the classification of wars, distinguishing them into ones of 'choice' and of 'necessity'. The chapter provides clear distinctions between the two. More importantly, the term 'Wars of National Survival' is introduced. This term may not be relevant in the contemporary global political scenario since it is highly unlikely that nation-states will face such moment of truth. However, the author feels that it is necessary to understand the nuances of this term for a simple and present-day reason. The primary terrorist organisation of today, the Islamic State, is in the throes of fighting for its very survival. An analysis of the concept of a war of national survival will be illuminating in terms of providing an indication of the future steps that it might initiate in its fight against the rest of the world. Currently the world has less than clear understanding of the options that it is considering and is groping in the dark.

The chapter also analyses the concept and conduct of irregular wars (IW). It explains three principles that bind the bounds of its normal conduct. The difficulties that conventional military forces have to overcome when faced with the necessity to engage in IW by adapting to the altered characteristics of the conflict are examined. The fundamental fact that the military forces of a nation are only one element that responds to an IW scenario is emphasised. Irregular forces, at least until now, only have limited air power capabilities whereas, the air power capabilities of the conventional force plays a critical role within the military response. An interesting development has been the concept of air denial, achieved through the employment of surface-to-air weapon systems, that is being considered by some of the irregular forces as an alternative to control of the air. However, this is an extremely short-term measure and not a viable concept for the future.

Politics is a critical influence in developing state behaviour. National security perceptions are almost a direct function of domestic political developments. Chapter 2 looks at the political influence on the development of air power capabilities of a nation. The current political environment does not permit the military to function independently even after parliamentary approval for its employment has been granted. For a number of reasons, there will always be political oversight of military campaigns. Essentially there is now an overlap of political and military responsibilities and they may not be fully aligned in some circumstances. Such a situation could lead to dissonance at the national level. The chapter goes on to bring out five implications of political influence on air forces of the nation.

Air power currently enjoys a status of primacy as a power projection capability within the elements of national power. The progression to this position has been assisted and enabled by technological innovations. Chapter 3 analyses the contribution of technology to air power development. It emphasises the challenge posed to air forces by air power needing to function at the cutting edge of technology in order to be effective. This scenario has a number of pitfalls for small and medium air forces. The requirements to be able accept leading-edge technology and operate sophisticated systems are multifarious and complex. They may not be within the reach of all air forces. Appropriate technology is resource-intensive, whether it is developed indigenously or acquired from allies. Not all nations will have the technology base to develop them or the necessary resources to support its acquisition. This situation will almost immediately and directly impact the quality of air power that a nation will be able to generate and sustain.

This chapter also debates the question of whether air forces should be developed as technologically high-end or low-end military forces. It is obvious that some dichotomies do exist when a capability is almost completely dependent on technology-led or–enabled developments.

Six major such dichotomies, which would continue to influence air power development in the future, are enumerated and explained.

In the past few decades, air power has become a capability that is generated by systems or even by systems of systems. It is not efficient to have single or multiple, but stand-alone, platforms apply air power. In this sphere, uninhabited aerial vehicles (UAVs) have become common-use platforms. Chapter 4 views the future of UAVs and explores the impact of the move towards creating autonomous systems. The legal, moral and ethical issues that seem to plague the use of artificial intelligence (AI) in the application of lethal force are many and need considerable and informed debate before being resolved. On the other hand, there is almost unanimous acceptance of the ubiquity of UAVs in the ISR role although large area surveillance is still beyond their capabilities. The persistence achieved by UAVs in the ISR role is localised and achieved after other more capable systems have delineated the area for surveillance. The future may be different. The chapter also explores the possible concepts of operation for the employment of uninhabited combat aerial vehicles (UCAVs) in a future air campaign, after autonomy and AI have matured jointly.

Air Forces are the primary repositories of national air power. However, in times of relative peace they will struggle to be adequately funded to meet all the demands place on them, especially in democratic nations. In appreciation of this reality, chapter 5 looks at four focal points that air forces must always monitor in order to stay strategically relevant to the nation—concepts, capabilities, people and organisation. The inherent processes within each of these focal points will contribute directly to the efficacy of an air force.

Air power is a foundational requirement to ensure national security. It is also the most agile for of force projection. However, the inherent volatility—in its generation and application—makes it a difficult capability to sustainably manage and optimise. A high order of professional mastery is required to harness the full potential of air power and apply it in a focused manner towards achieving national security imperatives. Such professional mastery comes with experience and dedicated study. There are no overnight solutions to achieve this.

Air power is, and will continue to be, a complex capability, but one that is critical to the well-being of a nation.

> 'In sum, the nature of air warfare and air power employment in this diffuse, increasingly interdependent and ever more complex world, is changing quickly. Rapidly developing capabilities are bringing with them growing responsibilities and obligations. Radical new thinking will be required if these challenges are to be met and mastered.'
>
> Air Commodore G B Vallance, RAF[2]

---

2 Vallance, Air Commodore G. B., 'The Changing Nature of Air Warfare', in Dr Richard P. Hallion (ed), *Air Power Confronts an Unstable World*, Brassey's UK (Ltd), London, 1997, p. xxiii.

Chapter 1

AIR POWER AND THE EVOLVING CHARACTER OF WAR

> 'We have before us the greatest task even faced by any generation on men in the fight to preserve peace. War, I say again, is no longer and evil. In this age it seems intolerable. There is nothing to be said in favor of war except that it is the lesser of two evils. It is better than appeasement of aggression, and it is far better than submission to tyranny and oppression, because without freedom and respect for human dignity, life would not be worth living.'
>
> George C. Marshal[1]

War is an indelible part of human history. History also demonstrates that the nature of war has not changed over the centuries—all wars have been fought to achieve political objectives through the use of force, and it has remained a fundamentally human endeavour. In other words, all wars are political, both in terms of the reason for their initiation as well as in laying down the desired end-state. However, the characteristics and conduct of war have been continually evolving. This never-ending process of evolution and development, which started from the earliest times in the history of mankind, has been influenced by a number of factors.

---

1 Marshal, George C., Memorial Day Address, Washington D.C., 1950; As quoted in Emme, Eugene M., *The Impact of Air Power: National Security and World Politics*, D. Van Nostrand Company Inc, Princeton, New Jersey, 1959, p. 419.

The major factors are—available technology; context in which the conflict is being conducted; and the cultural, behavioural, societal and religious ethos of the participants.

In broadly tracing developments in the history of war it is seen that for about two decades after the end of World War II, the conduct of war and its fundamental characteristics remained almost unchanged. Conflicts were almost always fought between the military forces of two or more sovereign nations that, by and large adhered to the accepted laws of armed conflict. However, with the advent of the Vietnam War in the 1960s, this status quo changed conclusively and forever. From the 1970s, a majority of conflicts have been fought with the legitimate military forces of a nation, or a coalition of nations on the one side and non-traditional, irregular adversaries on the other. Over the past fifty years, developments in the contemporary security scenario have impacted and changed the conduct of war. Today, the probability of a conventional state-on-state conflict taking place is extremely low.

In this monograph, the terms 'war' and 'conflict' have been used interchangeably. They only denote the employment of the military forces of a sovereign nation against adversaries who themselves may or may not constitute a regular military force affiliated to a nation. Although there is a distinction between the terms war and conflict, increasingly the term war is being commonly used to denote military operations and other lethal applications of force. However, it is noteworthy that no nation has declared 'war' on another for more than half a century. For example, during the Kosovo crisis in 1999, NATO mounted over 34,000 aerial sorties in 78 days against Serb forces and Belgrade and yet it was still not formally at war![2]

Viewed from a different perspective it becomes apparent that the fundamental reasons for the employment of military force, at the very base strategic level, have not changed noticeably for centuries. Military forces have always been used to secure the nation and its interests through the enforcement of a cycle of strategies. This cycle ranges from the benign concept of influence and shape through the strategies

---

2 Strachan, Hew, 'Introductory Essay: The Changing Character of War', in Karl Erik Haug & Ole Jorgen Maao (eds) *Conceptualising Modern War*, Columbia University Press, New York, 2011, p. 19.

of deterrence, coercion and the ultimate strategy of punishment and destruction. However, the employment of military forces, and air power within this overall capability, has altered considerably over the past decades because of two reasons. First, the capabilities of military forces are being continually improved and therefore are in a constant state of flux. Second, the characteristics and conduct of war have been evolving over the years along with the enhanced capabilities of the forces involved. These two factors are not mutually exclusive and form a remarkable and continuous cycle, of reasoned change in one bringing in a reactionary change in the other, and vice versa. The changes, in military capabilities as well as in the characteristics and conduct of war, do not occur at a constant rate and nor are they predictable with any level of assurance. However, there is no doubting the fact that the characteristics and conduct of war are constantly evolving and the capabilities of military forces are continually being enhanced.

The ascendancy of air power as an instrument of national power has been unprecedented in military history. When military competency across the full spectrum of conflict—encompassing the delivery on humanitarian aid and disaster relief on the one end to waging a war of national survival on the other—is considered to be a national necessity, air power emerges as a game-changing capability in a number of circumstances. However, despite the claims of over-zealous air power enthusiasts, it has never been, and never will be, the sole arbiter in winning a war. The changing characteristics and conduct of war reinforce this paradigm. In order to appreciate the further evolution of the conduct of war into the future, a few questions that have been thrown up with the introduction of irregular forces into the battlefield need to be answered in a considered manner.

Classifying Wars

The wars that a nation can embark upon can be classified broadly into two—either 'wars of choice' or 'wars of necessity'. This bifurcation will hold true irrespective of characteristics or conduct of the current and also future conflicts. Wars of choice are the ones in which the strategic national security imperatives and broader interests of the participating nation(s) will only be indirectly or peripherally influenced by the outcome of the conflict. They are also ones from which a nation can withdraw at will, even if the desired end-state has not been achieved, without any serious or long-lasting prejudice to national security.

Wars of necessity are different. They are conflicts that a nation is compelled to fight because not doing so would be directly detrimental to the overall well-being of the nation. Non-participation in such a war will ultimately impact on the independence and sovereignty of the nation. Further, the consequences of losing such a conflict could be dire and spans a very broad spectrum. Even at the lowest end of this spectrum, losing such a war could produce unpalatable security challenges and at the higher end it could even threaten the very existence of the nation. Even if such a war is not 'lost' but the outcome has been disadvantageous to a nation, there will be long-term consequences to the security situation of the nation concerned. At the high end of the spectrum, where 'wars of national survival' would be fought, are fortunately extremely rare occurrences. Even so, wars of necessity continue to be distinct possibilities. All nations must prepare for the eventuality that a war of necessity may have to be fought at some stage in its development.

The fact is that the global security environment has become more complex and exposed to the vagaries of actions by rogue states after the breakup of the Soviet Union and the end of the Cold War. This is indicated by the increased number of regional conflicts being fought in different parts of the world now as compared to the situation just two decades back. The Middle-East is currently going through its worst turmoil in history. However, from a Western perspective, all the on-going conflicts are wars of choice. In contemporary global politics, the default situation is that the democratic Western world bears the onus of responsibility to maintain the peace, and enforce it when required, in the hotspots around the world. The reasons for this situation are many and multi-faceted. The result is that these nations are therefore compelled to fight 'wars of choice' to stabilise volatile regions. The question that comes up is whether or not these 'wars of choice' have gradually crept into the lower levels of 'wars of necessity' since the prevalent instability in the volatile regions cannot be allowed to spread. Have the Western military interventions of the past two decades around the world been actually 'wars of necessity' for the more developed democratic nations? Both negative and positive answers could be logically argued, emphasising the complexity of global power projection. It also indicates the prevailing volatility of the global security environment.

The current indicators—evolving global security environment, the on-going conflicts around the world, rising anarchy in some regions, religious fundamentalism and intolerance that support violent extremism, sectarian divisions that invariably lead to violence, mass migration brought on by armed conflict, and the adoption of random acts of violence against innocent civilians as a tactic to further an ideological cause based on religion, politics or ethnicity—all point towards the entrenchment of the well-established trend for wars of the future to be irregular in its conduct and characteristics. It is highly unlikely that the world will witness the outbreak of a serious state-on-state conflict of any significance in the near to mid-term future.

However, the same cannot be said to be true of irregular warfare (IW). Irregular conflicts that have no fixed start point or end time, and which rapidly vary in its tempo and intensity will continue to manifest and fester in a number of regions. Although there is no assurance that conventional military forces of established democracies will always intervene when an irregular war erupts in any part of the world, the probability of such an intervention has become increasingly high in the recent past. At least for the foreseeable future military forces of the more developed world will be faced with the prospect of having to fight an irregular war in some remote and unstable part of the globe. In most cases, such an involvement will normally be as part of a coalition functioning under the aegis of the United Nations.

Irregular Warfare – Three Principles

In the prevailing geo-strategic environment, military forces of a sovereign nation will be forced to engage in irregular wars. Even in the volatile contemporary security environment, conventional wars adhere to certain accepted norms and characteristics. However, irregular wars will be conducted within very flexible and changeable principles and concepts. Even so, three very broad principles that are applicable to all irregular wars can be identified.

First is the permanency of the conflict. Irregular wars can erupt rapidly, even in stable nations. The reasons for the emergence of an irregular war are many and varied and is not germane to this discussion. Once an irregular war has set in, it blurs the distinction between a state of war and peace as understood in conventional thinking. The answer to the question, 'What is a state of war?' itself will vary in a nation where an irregular war is being fought. Since most irregular conflicts are the culmination of ideological discontent, the consequences of the conflict impact on social, political and economic well-being of the nation. Further, unless the ideological end-state is achieved, the conflict will not end. Permanency of the conflict, counted in terms of years rather than days or months, will be the result.

Second is that an irregular war is always multi-dimensional in its conduct. Like in any armed conflict, the participants in irregular conflicts also aspire to achieve strategic end-states. In order to do so, the combatants will strive to create strategic effects across all domains. This will require the employment of all elements of national power—economic, political and information. As a corollary, the irregular force will attempt to negate the effects that the conventional military forces can bring to bear through focusing on non-military means. The result will be a wider spread of the impact of irregular wars into different domains, relative to a conventional conflict.

The third principle is that success in an irregular war will depend on the ability of the state to conduct a whole-of-government campaign. The unified and optimised application of elements of national power is a foundational requirement for success. In addition, since irregular wars stem from a conflict of ideology, the strategic of influence and shape will have to be at the forefront of countering the irregular force. In this strategy, the role of military forces is only that of a facilitator and of support to the lead agencies. Historically, irregular wars have not been successfully contained by military actions alone, although the instinctive reaction of most governments at the onset of an irregular conflict is to employ the superior military power of the state to defeat the uprising. A carefully crafted whole-of-government approach is the only viable answer to mitigating the challenge of irregular wars.

In order to diffuse an irregular war, the state needs strategic depth in geographic territory, political acumen and economic strength. Lack of any of these will detract from the ability to contain and then defeat an irregular adversary.

Military Forces and Irregular Wars

Ever since World War II, the military forces of the Western nations have demonstrated overwhelming superiority in force projection capabilities and the quantum and destructiveness of fire power that they can bring to bear against an adversary. These capabilities tend to become demonstrably focused when applied in conventional battles and traditional theatres of operations. The outcome of this situation has been a gradual but pervasive shift in the conduct of war, irrespective of the nature of the two or multiple adversaries. When the adversary has acknowledged greater power than what is possessed by oneself, the trend has historically been to resort to asymmetry to neutralise the advantage of the adversary, to whatever degree possible. This trend has now manifest itself in the conduct of armed conflict and turned most of them into Irregular Wars.

It has now come to pass that almost all contemporary conflicts have assumed at least some of the characteristics of IW and there are almost no instances of purely 'regular' or conventional wars being fought. The adoption of non-traditional means to wage war by even a single participant in a conflict introduces the concept of asymmetry into it. The employment of asymmetry changes the character and conduct of the war irreconcilably. For the foreseeable future, all wars or conflicts that conventional military forces will be involved in, will have some form or the other of IW and one or more participant will be a non-state or sub-state actor(s).

Over the years irregular wars have been called by other names—small wars, low-intensity conflict, guerrilla war, asymmetric warfare etc.—however, none of these terms convey an understanding of the full spectrum of secondary and tertiary warfare that is associated with IW. In a sort of a reverse definition, IW could be considered to be all kinds of wars and conflicts other than state-on-state, military-versus-military encounters. The characteristics of any conflict are defined by the inherent capabilities, fighting ethos and operational concepts of the combatants and by their preferred modus operandi. This combined factor directly influences all analyses of IW. It is seen that the conduct of IW varies with a number of factors and is in a state of great flux most of the time. The innate asymmetry that comes with adopting the strategies, concepts and tactics that are germane to IW is an attractive prospect for non-state groups to adopt, especially when they lack sufficient conventional capabilities. By adopting and emphasising asymmetric concepts ad tactics they stand the chance of at least partially neutralising the, normally more dominant, military power of a sovereign state. This is one of the major reasons for almost all insurgencies to start as irregular wars.

At least for the foreseeable future, conventional military forces will be engaged in IW. However, they will simultaneously have to maintain the high-end capabilities necessary to fight and win conventional wars. The current trend suggests that conventional wars will invariably be wars of necessity and therefore will leave the military forces with almost no choice but to fight them. The sovereignty and integrity of the nation's geographic borders cannot be assured by any other means in the face of direct threats. The necessity to maintain high-end capabilities that can be adapted for the lower end of the spectrum of conflict is a tall order for air forces that are normally forced to function at the minimum level of capacity, mass and capability because of extraneous influences.

Regular, meaning traditional or conventional, military forces struggle to adapt to irregular conflicts since their doctrine, concepts, training and fundamental fighting ethos are oriented towards fighting an adversary organised in a similar manner as themselves. Although in the past two decades giant strides have been made by national military forces in adapting to the greatly changed conditions in which contemporary wars are being fought, the conduct of IW is still not a fully entrenched capability resident in regular military forces. However, the fundamental reason for the existence of a military force is to defend the nation against any and all attacks. This creates a quandary, which is double-edged. One is that only a numerically large military force with assured resource-availability will have the inherent capacity to train sufficient forces in the art of IW—the newfound characteristics and modus operandi associated with IW—while continuing to retain forces with adequate high-end capability. This would essentially mean creating and sustaining two differently capable forces within the same umbrella. Since most democratic governments have reduced the size and resource allocation of their military forces, cutting the fat close to the bone, it is highly unlikely that sufficient spare capacity, mass and resources will be available to most military forces to indulge in this luxury.

The second aspect flows from the first. The challenge is for numerically small military forces to be able to adapt quickly to the new paradigms of warfighting in the IW arena, while still being able to perform their core function. The core function involves the protection of national interests even if forced to enter wars of necessity against adversaries who may have both IW and conventional capabilities in equal measure. In simple terms, a conventional military force should be able to fight and win a war of necessity against an opposing national force who could bring to bear all conventional warfighting capabilities; and be also capable of containing subversive irregular forces simultaneously, to be able to fulfil its primary responsibility to the nation. This in turn would involve the force being agile enough to maintain high-end capabilities that are rapidly tailorable to the IW environment. This is the future and smaller military forces will find the dual demands placed on them extremely difficult to fulfil adequately, an unenviable situation to be in when national security is at stake.

Air Power in IW

The continual evolution in the conduct of war will be an ever-present criteria that will influence the development of air power capabilities. It becomes necessary to analyse the perceived roles that a middle power air force would be expected to fulfil, in the light of the changes in the conduct and characteristics of war. Meeting these expectations will be a critical factor for smaller air forces to continue to remain strategically influential in the national security equation. All mid-size and smaller air forces face the same major challenges—resource constraints, an ever-changing threat scenario, increased demands from the government to perform within a much broader spectrum of operations than ever before, difficulty in recruitment and retention of sufficiently qualified individuals, and longer duration expeditionary deployments that tend to directly impact operational preparedness at the basic level. Even though the challenges are common, there are no overarching solutions that could be adopted by all and any air force. A generic panacea for even one of the challenges is not a reality. They have to be solved independently and discretely in a contextual manner by each individual air force, taking into account the unique requirements of national security of the nation concerned.

Within this complex security environment, two factors exert almost over powering influence on the efficacy of the future employment of air power. First are the capabilities that must be inherent in an air force for it to become and continue to be strategically influential vis-à-vis national security. Only an air force with full-spectrum capability can achieve this status. An air force can be considered full-spectrum capable only if it can carry out all core and secondary air power roles at an adequately high level of competency and be able to sustain such application for the duration necessary to ensure national security. Further, it must also be capable of implementing the selected national security strategy to achieve the desired objectives. The core air power roles of control of the air, strike, air mobility and ISR as well as its enabling roles can only be conducted effectively by an air force only with appropriate and adequate resident combat capabilities. This statement needs elaboration, especially in relation to its veracity in an irregular conflict.

The raison d'etre of an air force is to ensure that the nation's surface forces are able to operate without undue interference from adversary air power at times and places of one's own choosing. This is control of the air. Such control of the air could be tailored in time and space and could also be graded in terms of the actual control that can be exercised—from air supremacy to a tolerable air situation at the other end. The requirement to control the airspace is overarching irrespective of the kind of war being fought and even if the adversary has only limited air power capabilities. Past history indicates that irregular adversaries normally do not possess air power of a high calibre. Therefore, the conventional military force almost always achieves control of the air very early in the conflict with relatively little effort. Even so, this scenario cannot be taken for granted into the future because of two recent developments.

One, a number of irregular forces are acquiring basic air power capabilities and it can be anticipated that this trend will manifest more acutely into the future. Two, the concept of control of the air is now being gradually nuanced to also incorporate the idea of air denial over a vital point or area. This is achieved through the employment of sophisticated surface-based air defence weapon systems. Defeating such systems require the possession of equally sophisticated systems. The necessity to possess the inherent capabilities to achieve effective control of the air, even when denial is being sought by the adversary, leads to the requirement for the air force to be able to operate at the leading edge of technology. It also needs to ameliorate the myriad issues that influence obtaining and maintaining adequate control of the air. Further, the other core roles that an air force will have to perform will also, off necessity, require an equal investment in sophisticated technology.

Considering the emerging security scenario, it must be accepted that air power will be involved in IW, irrespective of the size and composition of the irregular force and the availability or otherwise of its air power capabilities. However, there is a point, which is marginally outside the main thrust of this chapter to be considered. It pertains to the general perception of contemporary IW being totally land-centric operations where the infantry, the foot-soldier, carries the fight to the adversary through both rural and urban settings in remote and inaccessible regions of the world. This land-centric appreciation is not supported by the ground realities of contemporary conflict. It is air power that deploys the land forces to the theatre, sustains them through the deployment period, protects them from enemy aerial attacks, provides rapid response fire support when necessary, isolates the battlespace to stop external assistance to the adversary irregular force, and provides timely and adequate situational awareness. Further, it also extracts the force when required, while also providing aero-medical evacuation on an as required basis. It will not be wrong to state that air power is the lynchpin around which the land-centric IW campaign is built and sustained.

Even so, IW does tend to become land-centric, especially when the adversary forces have the capacity to merge effortlessly with the local population. This situation and the fact that most IW adversaries would not have any air power capabilities has brought about a perception within the land forces that only a small amount of 'integral air' is necessary to win the battle and campaign. This belief does not take into account the criticality of air power to provide assured control of the air; the extreme utility of air mobility, both intra- and inter-theatre; the total reliance on airborne ISR for the success of each mission; and the intense effectiveness of time-critical neutralisation of targets.

Successful IW campaigns have to be fought within the concept of a whole-of-government approach, in which all elements of national power have their individual roles to play. In the overall scenario, the military plays a significant role. Within this scenario, air power is not only critical, but irreplaceable. This is not to state that air power alone will be able to win an IW campaign. Far from it. A lot can be achieved by air power and by other force projection capabilities functioning independently, but victory in IW will only be achieved when a whole-of-government approach is adopted.

In the evolving contemporary battlespace, the air power capabilities of an air force would need to be adaptable to cater for the rapid changes that take place, at the strategic, operational and tactical levels. Such adaptation needs to be achieved in a short span of time, especially when applied in the context of an irregular war. In this case air power would have to be employed in a more nuanced and discrete manner. The ability of air power to detect, decide and defeat emerging threats with sufficient flexibility—through providing both lethal and non-lethal solutions—and discrimination can, if carefully tailored and employed 'intelligently', shift the asymmetry in favour of the conventional forces. In a subtle manner the inherent asymmetry resident in air power can be leveraged to neutralise the asymmetry that irregular forces employ as their primary tool. The question however is the extent to which air power capabilities can be shaped and skewed without creating a permanent convolution in the broader air power capability spectrum of an air force.

It will be possible for a sufficiently large air force to achieve the necessary flexibility and adaptability needed to cater for IW through the creation of a dedicated force oriented to function only within the capability spectrum needed to function in an irregular war scenario. Medium and small sized air forces will need to tread carefully in attempting this transformation since they would not have the spare capacity to dedicate purely to the conduct of IW. It therefore becomes necessary to ensure that the limited quantum of air power resident in these air forces have the built-in capacity to be rapidly adaptable to the requirements needed to fight and win the current campaign. Contextual adaptation will be the key to success. The air force would need to be effective in the most probable conflicts of the future, which would be irregular in nature, while retaining the ability to fulfil the fundamental responsibility of protecting the nation and its interests from conventional external attacks. This is the flexible capability and conceptual agility that will be demanded of an air force in the future.

In the future, the challenge of air power employment in IW would have to consider the core competencies that it brings to a particular campaign. The optimal employment of the available capabilities—individually or in appropriate combinations—would be the next step. Each IW campaign by its very definition will be unique in character and conduct. Air power practitioners will need to leverage the inherent flexibility of air power to maximise the effects that they can create. They must also be able to distinguish and tailor the effects to match the context. While precision strike, air mobility and ISR are the main capabilities that air power contributes, their availability and concerted application at the time and place of one's own choice will have to be ensured.

Control of the Air

In the employment of air power in conflict situations there is one area that is relatively easy to predict for the future—irrespective of any other demands that will be placed on air power, it will be primarily tasked to obtain and maintain control of the air, across the entire spectrum of conflict. Control of the air has long been accepted as a prerequisite for the smooth conduct and success of all other operations. Even though the fundamental concept of control of the air continues to be valid, the manner in which it is achieved is even today evolving. In the broader concept of control of the air, an emerging notion of air denial through the use of sophisticated surface-to-air weapon systems is also making its presence felt. The future development of this sub-concept will be worth watching, especially in the emerging IW scenario.

In a hybrid IW situation, control of the air will normally rest with the conventional force in the fray. However the emerging trend, the concept of air denial, could become more pronounced in the future. There has been some speculation and conceptualising that air denial could be substituted for control of the air, especially when the force concerned is short of air power capabilities. Constraints in resource availability could also make an irregular force consider this option. However, the concept does not stand up to a broader scrutiny. Air denial is the ability of a force to deny the use of a delineated airspace to the adversary through the deployment of ground-based air defences. This is a defensive concept and like most defensive initiatives can never be fully enforced in a foolproof manner. Air denial may work for a period of time, but the very nature of the concept is self-defeating when the contending force is proactively and offensively trying to achieve the necessary level of control of the air.

Surface-to-air weapons systems are relatively less expensive to procure. They are also relatively easier to operate. Deploying such systems could possibly achieve a fundamental level of air denial over a vital point or even area for a specific period of time. However, this is only a negation and will not provide the freedom to use the air medium for one's own purposes. Such freedom requires the capability to fight for, obtain and maintain the necessary level of control of the air within the desired time and space constraint. Surface-to-air missiles are not the equivalent of a poor man's air force and therefore even irregular forces that possess a few of these systems cannot be considered to have 'air power' capabilities. All the same, they may be able to disrupt air operations, for limited periods and in designated areas. This must be factored into the planning scenario, since air power has become the mainstay of conventional forces' response to IW.

The Perception Deficit

Even though air power has evolved into an extremely competent power projection capability, with the ability to function effectively across the entire spectrum of conflict, it has always suffered from a perception deficit. The reason for this can be traced back to the origins of air power becoming a military capability during World War I and the contentious debate that followed regarding its efficacy and independence. Perhaps as an instinctive protective measure, the proponents of air power tended to make over-ambitious claims of what air power could accomplish as a military capability. Some of the more extravagant claims have taken almost a century of technological and conceptual developments to come to fruition. This legacy has continued to plague futuristic thinking on air power. It follows that the analysis of any claim that is made regarding air power efficacy is tinged with scepticism even today. A perception deficit in the air power arena is clearly discernible. There are three aspects to this perception deficit from which air power suffers, much to its detriment.

First is the perception of impermanence that is generated in the minds of all concerned when an air campaign is conducted independently without the accompanying, and visible, presence of soldiers on the ground. This detracts directly from the efficacy of air power, especially when it is being employed in pursuance of the strategies of deterrence or coercion. Both these strategies rely on influencing the cognitive domain of the potential adversary to achieve the necessary level of effectiveness. A perception deficit regarding the capacity of air power to inflict the threatened damage will invariably lead to the failure of these strategies. In these circumstances perception management assumes the highest priority amongst all the issues that have to be addressed in the application of air power. Perception deficit is unlikely to be completely neutralised in the near term and therefore will remain a challenge for air power advocates and practitioners to mitigate.

The second is the unarticulated, but entrenched expectation regarding the accuracy of air attacks. There is an overwhelming demand that there should not be unintended casualties and other collateral damage even when extremely lethal weapons are employed. Even with the most precise weapons in use, the failure of intelligence could lead to the wrong target being attacked. The challenge of ensuring complete accuracy of intelligence is one that can never be fully ameliorated in an assured manner. In the prosecution of air attacks, there will always be fallibilities, whether it is in gathering intelligence, the targeting process or in the actual delivery of the weapon system. While these cannot be attributed as direct failures of air power, popular perceptions tend to make them so.

The third aspect originates since there is very little difference in the actual application of air power between conventional and irregular campaigns. Since only limited tactical changes are necessary for air power to function optimally in the IW scenario, the air force is not 'seen' to be 'preparing' for a conflict as such. However, the same changes in the conduct of the conflict and subsequent alteration of the combat scenario brings about sweeping changes to the fundamental concept of operations of a conventional army. The air force on the other hand is capable of going into the fight almost immediately. The general opinion therefore is that an air force is only peripherally important to an IW campaign. This opinion contributes to the overall perception deficit. The fact of air power being flexible in the extreme and contributing enormously to all aspects of IW is lost in translation.

Conclusion

The emerging scenario is this: the probability of a full-fledged state-on-state conflict taking place is fairly low; in order to remain strategically influential as a critical element within the national security calculus, air forces need to possess full-spectrum capability; the same capabilities need to be contextually flexible in order to be equally effective in both traditional and non-traditional, irregular wars; and air power will have to continue to manage the wrong perceptions that have become entrenched in the broader society regarding the efficacy of its application. Air denial through the employment of surface-to-air missile systems can at best provide a respite from air attacks, and will normally be limited in time and space. It can never be a viable alternative concept that replaces control of the air.

It will be an ill-judged move by a smaller air force to sacrifice the capabilities required to carry out its core role of control of the air to expeditiously ensure that the peculiar demands of irregular wars are met. The unchanging need as air forces focus on the wars of the future is to ensure that they retain strategic influence in the national security calculus. Air Forces are inherently strategic in nature and at the fundamental level meant for the protection of the nation and its interests. It has to be ensured that air forces are not reduced to being tactical tools in the urgency to meet emerging irregular threats. The future will belong to air forces that have strategic agility and are supported by governments that understand the implications of not being in possession of high calibre air forces in the rapidly changing global geo-political and security environment.

'In short, air power is, and will remain, quintessentially a necessary, though not sufficient, condition for conflict resolution. Inflated expectations have led to the denigration of air power because it cannot impose a favourable result in volatile political and strategic environments with underlying dynamics that are impervious to any kind of armed force. Air power may contribute to conflict resolution, but its effects must relate to the broader political-military characteristics and nature of the specific conflict.'

John Olsen[3]

---

3   Olsen, John Andreas in 'Introduction' in John Andrea Olsen (ed), *European Air Power: Challenges and Opportunities*, Potomac Books, USA, 2014, p.xviii,

Chapter 2

POLITICS AND AIR POWER

'Wars and conflicts are conducted at four levels – political, strategic, theatre and tactical – with each level sitting within the context of the other, in descending order for the political;...The first, political level, is the source of power and decision. This level has always existed in that armies enter combat not merely because two or more of them happen to be hanging around an empty battlefield and decide to fill in some time but because an issue between two or more political entities cannot be settled in other ways and therefore military means are resorted to.'

Rupert Smith[4]

The future is full of uncertainties, the aphorism that change is the only constant is perhaps aptly applied to the consideration of the future. Even so, from an air power perspective it can be safely stated that its future employment will always be dictated by political developments—both domestic and international. Politics is a critical influence on the behaviour of a nation, especially when the employment of its military forces is being considered as an option to mitigate emerging security challenges. In an overarching assessment of the global security situation, it could be assumed with an acceptable level of assurance that military forces of the democratic world will continue to be pressed into service to stabilise volatile regions. Within

---

4 Smith, Rupert, *The Utility of Force: The Art of War in the Modern World*, Penguin Books, London, 2006, pp. 10-11.

this calculus it can also be presumed that air power would continue to be employed in similar geo-strategic situations as is currently prevalent. However, the modus operandi will continue to evolve with the introduction of new technology and accompanying changes to concepts of operation.

At the strategic level, air forces are only as relevant to national security as the effectiveness of their capabilities in achieving laid down national objectives. The resident air power capabilities will be employed to ensure that national security imperatives are met and national interests protected. National objectives and the priorities allocated to each of them are stipulated by the government of the day and are direct products of the political beliefs and security perceptions of the nation. In turn, the air power capabilities that a nation must, or should, possess will be determined by the prioritised national security requirements as envisaged by the government.

Political factors that affect acquisition, sustainment and employment of air power have different iterations. It would be naïve on the part of air power planners to believe that air power will be employed in isolation to other government agencies, especially in democratic nations. Further, there can be no doubt that the desired end-state in any conflict, irrespective of the actual modus operandi, will always be defined at the political level. This is as it should be. The employment of military forces to further national interests must always be underpinned by strategic political directives.

Within the overall military posture of a nation, the ability of air power to respond rapidly to a broad range of emerging scenarios is highly prized. This unique ability also clearly distinguishes it from other, more lumbering, power projection capabilities. Air power further embellishes its rapid response capability with precision, discrimination and proportionality in its application of lethal force and the creation of the desired effects. The downside is that the very same capabilities build-up extraordinarily high expectations of air power, which could at times become a burden too heavy to shoulder. This disadvantage could impact the performance envelope of smaller air forces more than the larger ones, since they may not have sufficient depth of capabilities within the force to avoid failure. Perception management becomes a high priority activity in these circumstances.

There is a distinctive factor that defines the relationship between air power and the political influence on its application. Understanding this delicate relationship is relatively more important for air power professionals than for the lay person. In the past few decades a clear trend towards increasing political oversight and 'interference' in the actual conduct of military operations can be observed. In the case of the employment of air power, its greater media visibility makes political interference a certainty. Such oversight can become highly intrusive from the perspective of commanders and operators. These intrusive interferences will almost always prove to be detrimental to the optimised and effective application of air power. This is so since the intervention in the command, and at times operational, processes will invariably be done by non-professionals with limited knowledge regarding the nuances of the application of air power. The demands placed on air commanders in such situations to balance the political requirements while simultaneously ensuring the efficacy of air power will be enormous.

Unfortunately in the contemporary political climate the delineation of political and military responsibilities in the conduct of a military campaign is not always easily made. Therefore, interfering political oversight even at the operational level, the proverbial long screw-driver, cannot be avoided. Air power professionals have to come to terms with the fact that political oversight, at times of an intrusive nature, will continue into the future. Future air power professionals have to be adept at balancing the need to keep the political leadership in-the-loop while ensuring that operational freedom of action and effectiveness are not diluted.

Considerable political influence will continue to be brought to bear on air forces in all future wars and conflicts. From a future perspective of the application of air power, political oversight will have five main implications emerge, that would be enduring. The employment of air power, now and into the future, would have to be undertaken with due cognisance of these factors.

Implication – First-choice Response Option

Air power is perhaps the most visible form of force projection. It is also able to readily adapt its inherent characteristics to ensure rapid and scalable application. When combined, these two facets of air power together creates a proclivity within the political leadership to turn to air power as the first-choice response option when faced with imminent hostilities or other amorphous threats to the nation. The employment of air power as an immediate response to provide humanitarian aid and disaster relief in times of both natural and man-made calamities is now almost routine. The reasons for this primacy given to air power are relatively simple. First, in the contemporary global politico-security environment, military interventions based on ground incursions invariably tend to have a high probability of own forces' casualties. This is politically untenable. Further, ground conflicts are unfortunately prone to mission-creep that in turn leads to the campaign dragging on for a far greater time than was initially envisaged. A protracted ground campaign has its own drawbacks and is something that all political leadership want to avoid. The ability of air power to mitigate these challenges automatically makes it the first-choice response option when power projection is required.

Second, air power has tremendous destructive power, if lethal force has to be used. More importantly, it has the inherent ability to rapidly scale up or down both the tempo and intensity of its application, almost at will. Therefore, it is relatively easier to meet the requirements of proportionality and discrimination when air power is being employed in a conflict. Third, curtailing and withdrawing from an air campaign is relatively faster as compared to disengaging and removing ground forces that have been in a theatre of operations for a length of time. A normal shut down of a boots-on-the-ground campaign takes far longer than closing down an air campaign. If the withdrawal has to be effected without any overt loss of stature to the withdrawing force, a ground withdrawal could take even longer. Air power does not suffer from these disadvantages.

As the first-choice response capability to an emergent politico-security and/or geo-strategic challenge to national security, air power provides both kinetic and non-kinetic options to the Government. The options that air power provides will depend on two factors—the overall capability resident in the extant air force; and the capability balance that it has managed to maintain in terms of systems availability and the quantum of air power that they are capable of generating. It is increasingly obvious that kinetic application of force is seen as a last resort action, even when the nation is involved in a conflict. On the other hand, the political and diplomatic initiatives of a nation can be bolstered through the nuanced employment of air power in an 'air-diplomacy' role. Air diplomacy can be described as the use of non-kinetic air power capabilities to further national security interests. This is done by leveraging the ample soft power resident in air power to complement other non-military efforts being made by the nation. This fits seamlessly into the whole-of-government approach to national security, predominantly in the pursuance of the strategies of influence and shape, deterrence, and coercion. Credibility of air power in the future will depend on the air force being able to maintain a credible balance between the ability to project soft and hard power.

The future employment of air power in most of its roles and in almost all circumstances, will depend on the satisfactory mitigation of a number of issues. The government will have to consider them at the apex political body before a decision is made to employ air power, even in its most benign mode. The major issues that need debate and clarification are—the legality of the application of lethal force and/or the intrusive employment of non-lethal air power capabilities, even when the emerging situation warrants the rapid provision of humanitarian aid; the international political and security environment as well as the opinion of other regional and global powers regarding the legitimacy of such an intervention; the acceptability of the action being contemplated within the domestic societal and political environment of the nation; and the resilience of the national economy to accept the financial implications of the actions being contemplated. These issues have to be satisfactorily answered, within the broader ethos of the nation, before the decision to employ air power can be taken.

Intervention in another nation, whether for benign reasons or for reasons of national security, whether through the application of lethal force, non-kinetic action or the provision of aid, is a complex endeavour and cannot be, must not be, decided upon on a whim. Military intervention has to be a considered action. This is a salutary lesson that comes across from a study of the history of military interventions. Future interventions will therefore, have to follow a process of strict evaluation and acceptance of necessity at the highest levels of government. Even so, the fact remains that across the spectrum of operations—from the provision of humanitarian aid to the conduct of armed conflict—effective air power provides an attractive option by being able to create disproportionately large effects while creating a minimal footprint in alien soil. It is therefore not surprising that governments that have ready access to such air power almost always use it as a first-choice response option. This trend will only get entrenched into the future.

There is no doubt regarding the criticality of air power in a joint and/or combined operation, undertaken by the military and other elements of national power. Within the military, by virtue of its status as the first-choice response option, air power will also be the one that is most often used in conjunction with other elements of national power. Such usage, within a whole-of-government approach to security, will only continue to increase in the future. This requires air campaign planners to have an acute awareness of the strategic objectives to be achieved and to ensure that the application of air power is always aligned with prioritised national objectives. While the need for this alignment may seem obvious, the strategic air power planning process needs to create a process to ensure it. The requirement is to create subsets of strategic objectives for the operational and tactical levels because of the unique tenet of air power employment—centralised control and decentralised execution. Air power is optimally applied when it is centrally controlled and executed in a decentralised manner. This approach ensures the conservation of high-end capabilities that are resource-intensive and therefore scarce. This unique requirement makes air power missions particularly vulnerable to being misaligned from the higher level objectives. The increasing stand-alone capabilities of air power systems make them more susceptible to this pitfall and therefore greater vigilance in planning, at all levels, is warranted in the planning and execution of a future air campaign.

Implication – Collateral Damage

The second political issue is the extremely complex challenge of limiting collateral damage in the application of force. Even as late as the 1970s, collateral damage was an accepted—even though reluctantly—fallout of waging war. Currently the situation is very different. While the Laws of Armed Conflict (LOAC) have not changed in the past few decades, the tolerance for collateral damage is at an all-time low. This is the result of two essential truths that seem to have been forgotten or ignored over a period of time. In a discussion of the application of air power and the political influences that envelope it, these realities must be articulated as precursors or caveats before analysing the current attitude towards collateral damage. One, no regular military force goes out of its way to create damage that is not warranted or necessary to achieve its stated objectives—in other words collateral damage in almost all cases is just that, the unintended consequence of the lethal application of force during times of conflict. The operative word in that statement is 'unintended', wanton destruction of all kinds has always been condemned.

Two, the internationally recognised LOAC does not state that the application of military force must always be done with the assurance of zero collateral damage. The LOAC only states that the concept of proportionality must be considered as the link between military necessity and humanity; the damage caused and the suffering inflicted should not be disproportionate to the military need; and a commander must weigh the possibility and amount of collateral damage against the advantage gained in targeting a legitimate military objective. This effectively means that a certain amount of collateral damage is not only unavoidable, but also acceptable within the ambit of international law, as long as necessary precautions are taken to ensure that such damage is kept within reasonable limits.

Despite this unambiguous position of the LOAC, collateral damage has become a politically noxious factor in all conflicts. The current situation is such that even marginal errors in the application of force that lead to minimal collateral damage have become contentious, if not unacceptable in an outright manner. One of the consequences has been greater political scrutiny of military operations, even down to the tactical level. There has to be clear understanding at the political level that the entire cycle of events, from arriving at the decision to apply lethal force to the actual delivery of the weapon, is prone to fallibility. The intelligence gathering and targeting process, as well as the actual delivery of the selected weapon can never be made infallible and fool-proof. This is a fact of military operations. In the cotemporary scenario however, even a miniscule amount of fallibility has become unacceptable to the political leadership in democratic nations. In these circumstances, the repercussions of accruing collateral damage will be far-reaching. It will lead to the curtailment of the necessary flexibility afforded to field commanders. Lack of flexibility will in turn directly compromise the efficacy of the application of air power. This scenario is already a reality in a number of instances and will become further entrenched as the pendulum of political correctness swings away from military necessity.

In a somewhat dichotomous manner, there is acceptance of the vicarious nature of military operations, while collateral damage has become the primary political focus in considering the application of lethal force, through the employment of military forces. Aversion to collateral damage and the call for zero tolerance has been raised to the status of an inviolable political code. This trend manifests most vehemently when military forces are engaged in irregular wars. There is a modicum of understanding within a whole-of-government approach to military interventions that lead to irregular wars that it is necessary to get the local population aligned with the intervening forces. In turn, civilian casualties and the damage or destruction of civilian, and even dual-use, infrastructure has become unacceptable in the current socio-political environment. The other side of the coin is that the conduct and characteristics of war have changed so much that even tactical actions taken in the battlefield can, and do, have immediate and powerful strategic consequences. A classic demonstration of this direct connection between tactical military actions and rapid strategic fall-out can be seen from an episode in November 2009 that took place in Afghanistan. An air attack on a stolen fuel bowser resulted in the death of a large number of Afghan 'civilians' in Kunduz. At the time of the attack, the pilot was unaware of the presence of civilians around the bowser who were siphoning off fuel. The consequence however was the resignation of the German Minister for Defence, almost as an atonement for the 'mistake'.

This assured strategic repercussion that all collateral damage brings with it has made the political leadership demand that all operations are undertaken with the assurance of absolute freedom from even the slightest collateral damage. Planning and successfully executing an air campaign has never been more complicated. This political constraint is unlikely to be removed and therefore air forces around the world would have to per force tailor their strategy, operational norms, tactics, rules of engagement and concepts of operation to meet the 'no-collateral damage' political expectation.

The moral and ethical condemnation that has become inextricably attached to collateral damage, portrayed through the ever-present lens of instant media criticism, is unlikely to change in the future. Collateral damage would perhaps become acceptable only in cases where the military forces are engaged in a war of national survival when political considerations, hopefully, are unlikely to restrict the use of military forces to their fullest and most lethal extent.

The unsavoury political fallout from collateral damage manifests in an increasing reluctance of governments to apply lethal force. This disinclination to apply lethal force, at times even in instances where it is warranted, has a direct impact on the development of future concepts of operation. This is particularly visible in the case of air campaigns in irregular wars where the demarcation between combatants and non-combatants are difficult to clearly distinguish. As IW is becoming more common and air power continues to be employed in difficult circumstances, it will be necessary to reemphasise air power's non-lethal capabilities. Its ability to carry out time-sensitive intelligence, surveillance and reconnaissance can be leveraged to establish a sufficiently strong deterrence posture in support of national security. When this is combined with precision strike, the effect increases exponentially. The non-kinetic capabilities of air power will become more pronounced in their usage in contemporary and future confrontational situations, especially in a climate where unintended human casualties and destruction of infrastructure are becoming increasingly unattractive to the political leadership.

An air campaign also suffers from the challenge of perception management. More often than not there is condemnation, most of the time created by the media, of air strikes being primarily responsible for the majority of collateral damage in a war zone. This is a wrong but popular perception. There is a media proclivity to provide extraordinarily graphic coverage to illustrate collateral damage suffered as a result of air strikes, as opposed to equal damage or even greater destruction created by other military actions such as artillery fire or a concentrated firefight between land units. This is a perception management challenge that is continually whittling away at the demonstrated efficiency of the lethal application of air power.

Implication – Resources

In an established democracy, resource allocation for the various needs of the nation is always politically controlled. It is an accepted fact that no nation, however rich, has sufficiency in resources to meet all the diverse demands that are placed on its economy. Therefore, the allocation and availability of resources to the military forces as a whole and within it to the development of air power and air forces become a direct function of political decisions. This decision-making cycle sits somewhat outside the control of the military and air forces. A purely academic analysis will invariably prove that in relative terms air power is more 'expensive' to acquire, employ and sustain than other forms of force projection. While this may indeed be true, it is only one part of the equation. The perception of this resource-intensive nature needs to be balanced with a detailed analysis of the inherent characteristics of air power, which makes it a uniquely flexible capability critical for national power projection. Only a cost-benefit analysis will provide a true picture of military capabilities that should be taken as the basis for resource allocation. In times of relative peace this entire process will become a difficult exercise to conduct in a meaningful manner. The political constraints that create the challenge of adequacy of resource allocation for air power will always remain, well into the future.

The other side of the coin is the need to manage public and political perception that air power is an expensive capability to maintain and employ. Yes, capable air forces that can field state-of-the-art air power are expensive to acquire, train, maintain, sustain and operate as viable forces and elements of national power. However, the perception of being resource-intensive is one-sided and does not take into account the multiple capabilities that an air force brings to bear across the entire spectrum of operations. Air forces need to articulate and emphasise the fact that in a deliberate cost-benefit analysis, they are indeed highly cost-effective in comparison to some other elements of national power. They are also perhaps the most versatile of all national power elements. In a wide range of circumstances, air power offers the government credible and effective options to shape the environment, influence the adversary's behaviour, and manipulate emerging events in one's own favour without the commitment of major military force elements. There will be continuing need to influence and alter the perception of air power being far too expensive if it has to find its own position of influence within the security strategy of the nation. The future will only increase the resource allocation pressure on the development of air power. While there is no quick fix solution to this challenge, it has to be constantly monitored and ameliorated.

Implication – Morality

During times of relative peace, technological developments and refinements in weapon systems almost always lead concept development. There is a stream of development currently taking place, which must be considered for thought and discussion—the employment of non-lethal ordnances as part of air delivered weapon systems. Non-lethal ordnances are meant to debilitate personnel so that they are incapable of undertaking combat operations by effectively incapacitating them for a pre-planned and specified duration. Even though such measures would be temporary in nature, such actions directly raise the question of morality in 'maiming' a person. Laser beams are already capable of blinding people and can be used even by individual soldiers. While such usage itself may be morally questionable, a broader question emerges. What would be the morality acceptance of using, say for example, an agent that causes blindness in all living beings within a designated area? Area-wide effects will, of necessity, have to be delivered through air power systems. Although currently a hypothetical question, this is perhaps one example of the moral dilemma that is bound to arise as and when such ordnances become operationally available to air forces.

Debates and disagreements regarding morality and ethics of the use of force had never been far from the surface in the conduct of war in the 20th century. It has become even more vociferous and contentious in the current scenario of IW. The complexity increases with wars being fought by proxy by and against combatants who even deny that they are combatants. The fact that the current adversaries of the Western nations do not subscribe to the same ethos of morality and ethics in battle makes this debate provocative and at time incomprehensible. Air power application is caught in the middle of this debate—one that can never categorically decide the right or wrong of the application of lethal force. Political decisions will influence the manner in which an air force confronts the dilemma regarding the ethical correctness and morality of the application of air power in any context. Even though it is necessary to have a debate and awareness of the challenges to morality within the force, the issue needs to be raised and settled at the national level. This is a necessity, particularly for the future, since the nation at large will look for explanations from the operators regarding the morality and ethics of their actions. A nationally accepted position regarding the moral and ethical correctness in the application of lethal military force is fundamental to the assured performance of the armed forces.

Implication – Coalition Operations

The global geo-political and economic environment makes it necessary to form coalitions before launching a military campaign. At the very base of this vital necessity are political compulsions that force the world's great powers to seek coalition partners to participate in their military adventures. The fundamental reason is essentially to ensure that there is international legitimacy as well as consensus and approval for the action being initiated. The need for legitimacy, bestowed by the participation of a large number of nations even in token form, is a paramount consideration in most cases. The more the coalition partners, more the legitimacy. In recent times coalitions are being put together either with the sanction of the United Nations or being gathered by a great power to pursue its own agenda. In the case of a middle or small power initiating the creation of a coalition, the reason may be more pragmatic with the coalition being created to ensure sufficiency of military power to achieve the desired objectives. In either case, smaller powers being asked to join a coalition will find it easier to commit air power to the group endeavour, rather than provide combat troops. By the very nature of their formation, coalitions are invariably political in nature. Irrespective of the reason for forming the coalition, it is almost certain that in contemporary operations air power is likely to be the first to be deployed.

Coalition operations bring with it a number of demands on air power that may not have been as important in the case of stand-alone independent operations. The fundamental requirement is for an air force to have sufficient interoperability with other partner air forces within the coalition. Since functioning within a coalition is almost completely political, achieving interoperability also has a political aspect to it. Commonalty of technology between partner nations is the by-product of political and diplomatic closeness between nations.

From a coalition perspective, finding commonality at the technical level is normally achieved by recognising the lowest common denominator, in other words the least technologically advanced force within the coalition, and then the entire coalition functioning at that level. In the case of air power this approach may not always work. Air power being a technology-enabled combat power, it is necessary for all capable air forces to function above a baseline technological capability. Any force functioning below that fundamental level would be more a burden than an asset within the coalition. Therefore, it is necessary for smaller air forces to continually update the level of technological sophistry and technical proficiency of the force.

This necessary update comes at a price at two levels. First, the real finances required to maintain the level of technology may become prohibitive for smaller economies. At some point in the quest for finances, the questions regarding the advisability and/or necessity of maintaining a combat oriented air force with its recurring costs will start to be asked and debated. This is a contextual argument and the answers and decisions will depend on the nation's perception of itself vis-à-vis its immediate neighbours, its actual and perceived security needs, and perhaps most importantly the socio-economic situation and cultural ethos of the nation. Second, the availability of technology to smaller air forces, which is a direct function of the political and diplomatic status of the nation. In both cases, the decision will be completely politically motivated although it will be the air force that pays the price for the decisions.

Another reason that will force an air force into a coalition network is the difficulty—in terms of resources and availability of technology—in maintaining a fully balanced force with sufficient depth in all capability envelopes. This would mean having a force with sufficient high-end capabilities that can be flexibly ramped down to a lower level when required. The deciding point is influenced by the political acceptance of this requirement. The high-end capabilities of air power are becoming so expensive that only a few air forces will be able to afford them in the quantum required to be self-sustaining. The option for most air forces is either to become 'niche' forces, which has its own list of challenges, or to retain a balanced structure with lesser quantum of capabilities across the spread. The second option, definitely the better of the two, would mean having to function with lesser depth than would be optimal if the air force is forced to operate on its own. It will also mean the acceptance in these forces that in the future they would operate within a coalition of allies and like-minded nations. From a sole consideration of the sovereignty of the nation, this may not be palatable, but will there be much of a choice in the future?

Conclusion

In straight terms, the capability of a national air force will be in direct proportion to the nation's international political standing. From a purely air force viewpoint the challenge of the future will be to maintain a force that is capable of accepting advanced technology transfers while being able to continue operations at the required tempo and intensity. This in turn will require the force to be maintained at a small percentage above the bare critical mass necessary for it to function at its optimum. Whether or not a nation maintains such a force will always be a political decision. Hopefully the decision will be based on a cohesive analysis of perceived threats to national security and the ability of the nation to procure and afford the necessary capabilities. The affordability and availability of technology—both directly influenced by political decisions—are the starting points for the development of the future air force.

Political influence will also manifest in terms of the rules of engagement within which an air force functions. These rules will always be more restrictive than the prevailing LOAC. In contemporary conflicts that are being waged against irregular forces who do not adhere to the internationally accepted norms of the conduct of war, the restrictiveness of national rules of engagement at times detract from the optimised application of air power. It is critically necessary for national air forces, and other military forces, to adhere to the LOAC at all times in order to continue to function from a higher moral plane than the irregular forces that they combat. However, rules of engagement that further restrict the application of air power could unduly impede the creation of the desired effects, to the detriment of achieving success. Future conflicts where this dichotomy gets further emphasised will probably need a reconsideration of the imposition of restrictive rules of engagement on air power elements. Adopting this stance will have to be a considered political decision.

In future, irrespective of the situation and the context for the application of air power, political directives are likely to become further stringent and could even curtail the freedom of operations that the inherent flexibility of air power provides to planners and executors. In these circumstances, it becomes extremely important to clearly define the limits within which air power can be applied and to make political decision-makers fully aware of what is achievable and what is not. Professional mastery at the strategic leadership level within an air force has never been more important than now and to ensure the relevance of air power into the future.

Chapter 3

THE CHALLENGE OF CUTTING-EDGE TECHNOLOGY

> 'The requirement from technology is simply this; it must improve the ability of the air force to perform its tasks at an economical price both in manpower and finance.'
>
> Sir Fredrick Rosier[5]

Air power has faced some fundamental challenges throughout the course of its development to arrive at its current status of primacy in power projection capabilities. The journey has not always been smooth or without interruption, but at the same time it has been one of continuous improvements in doctrine, capability, concepts and application. Through its developmental history, air power has been defined in multitudinous ways and has assumed different meanings and nuanced connotations in different nations and their military forces. Even so, there are two factors that have been universally agreed—that air power is technology-based and dependent; and it is resource-intensive, in a number of ways, to acquire, apply and sustain. As a corollary, the same two factors also become fundamental challenges to the smooth and progressive development of air power.

At the peril of repeating a cliché, it can be stated that air power is born off technology, has achieved its preeminent position through the

---

5 Rosier, Sir Fredrick, 'The Implications for Air Power of Development in Aircraft and Weapon Technology (I): The Operational View', in Feuchtwanger, DR E. J., & Mason, Group Captain, R. A., *Air Power in the Next Generation*, The Macmillan Press Ltd, London, 1979, p.95.

innovative application of cutting edge technology, and is technology-reliant for its sustainment. High-end technology is the lifeline that supports and maintains air power and permits its optimum application across the entire spectrum of military operations. In order to achieve the desired level of proficiency an air force must have the capability to assimilate and operate systems that are technically highly developed. Further, an air force needs to have an inherent technology orientation at all levels to fully exploit both extant and emerging capabilities. These demands require the force to encompass a number of disparate factors such as education and training of the work force, national technology base etc. The challenge for air forces, now and into the future, will be to reach a level of competence and have the inherent capacity thereafter to continue to maintain that position as long as required with full assurance. While this is a tall order, it is made more complex by the need to achieve it while encompassing the full spread of air power capabilities. These are undeniable challenges and airmen should be comfortable in articulating them. The very same challenges make it imperative for an air force to be fully capable of accepting technology and operating highly sophisticated systems. This capability is a cornerstone to ensuring the relevance and effectiveness of an air force to be a crucial element within the broader military capabilities of the nation.

There are two main factors that must be considered when analysing the ability, or otherwise, of an air force to accept and effectively employ cutting edge technology—the national education base, and the level of technology-acceptance.

National Education Base

The greatly increased bias towards sophisticated technology in the application of modern air power creates its own issues. First, it requires a technologically trained workforce at the commensurate level of knowledge and in adequate numbers to efficiently operate the advanced systems that generate air power. In order to generate this, the nation must have a sufficiently large pool of people with a minimum level of technological education from which the air force can recruit its own workforce for further advanced and specialised education and training. This further goes back to the status of the education system of the nation, which should be of a high enough standard to create a base of technology friendly and scientifically oriented personnel. While the national education base is a foundational requirement, the air force itself should have its own training and education processes to mould this available pool to the desired level of capacity. The fundamental demography of the nation will determine the sophistication and efficacy of its air force.

Maintaining and operating sophisticated, state-of-the-art air power assets require a high level of technical expertise and technological awareness within the workforce. A technologically advanced workforce is a prerequisite for the air force to enhance its capabilities. The other side of the coin is that a lack of focus on technical educational at the national level will gradually percolate into the air force. Irrespective of the in-house training and educational facilities that are provided, a low level of national technical education will translate to a commensurate dilution of technical competencies in the air force. Given financial sufficiency and adequate political and diplomatic influence, it will be easy enough for a nation to purchase modern air power equipment and systems from its allies. But converting them into sustainable air power capability is a completely different matter. Even a cursory look at the history of air forces will clearly bring out case studies of air forces who acquired high-technology systems but were neither able to maintain them at the required standards nor employ the inherent capabilities of the systems to any lasting effect. A robust and fundamentally advanced national level education is a crucial key to technological competence and the overall success of an air force. There can be no substitute for a workforce of calibre.

Level of Technology-Acceptance

Technology-acceptance capability is another challenge that most air forces face, perhaps more so than the other two arms of the military force. This is particularly relevant to air forces that are not self-sufficient in the research, development and manufacture of air power systems. In the late 20th and early 21st century, technology has moved forward at a relentless speed, and will continue to do so into the foreseeable future. At times the pace of advance is seen to be far too great for the process of development of the concepts of employment to keep up. This has the potential to create a situation where a particular advance in technology could become redundant and replaceable by another more enhanced one before it has even been properly evaluated and fielded by the operators. While this is a wonderful situation to be in, it is also a double-edged sword, especially for smaller air forces.

In terms of technology-acceptance, smaller air forces are impacted by the issues and repercussions that emanate from the challenge of having to operate at their critical mass almost constantly. First, a smaller air force will not normally have sufficient strategic or operational depth to absorb the loss of capability and capacity that a failure of technology will bring about. This failure could be that of the technology itself or that of the force to accept the technology. In both cases, the end-result will be the same—loss of overall capability. In other words, a failure will lead to the reduction in the overall air force capacity to function at the required level of competence and efficiency. A failure of technology itself can be avoided by ensuring that a smaller air force adopts technology that is a step behind the cutting edge. They should only look to induct technology that have already been proven in other larger air forces. The failure of technology-acceptance procedure in a smaller air force is much more serious. Such a failure points to the inadequacy of the education and training process of the air force and should be mitigated through concerted action. Technology-acceptance failure will translate immediately to the air force not being able to deliver the necessary capabilities at the required levels. This situation is the first step in a downward spiral.

Second, while the fact that smaller air forces function at their critical mass is inherently true, the very same constraint will force a smaller air force to become more adept at technological innovations that, in turn, will enhance the capability spectrum of the force as a whole. The combination—of functioning at critical mass but needing to innovate to enhance capabilities—is a volatile mix and must be carefully balanced. Further, technological innovations must be brought about while taking into account the obvious pitfalls of being completely at the cutting edge. Smaller air forces need to be cognisant of these complexities, but must create the capacity to innovate within the broad guidelines. The situation is unlikely to change in the medium-term future, and will only become increasingly complicated. Smaller air forces will always have to content with this dichotomy, and contain it in order to ensure success.

The state of the national industrial base is another factor that will influence the technology-acceptance capacity of an air force. The reality in the contemporary world is that highly sophisticated technology-based air power systems can be bought off-the-shelf if a nation has the wherewithal to pay for it. However, an indigenous aerospace industry of a minimum calibre is necessary to fully harness the capability that these systems bring. More importantly, an industry base is necessary to ensure their long term sustainability and viability. Richard Hallion makes this point very succinctly when he states, 'Because of the inherently complex nature of aerospace science and technology, air and space power requires the maintenance of a robust aerospace industrial base, one that supports both civil and military aircraft development, for civil and military aeronautics are inextricably linked.'[6] There are any number of examples of smaller air forces having purchased high-end air power systems and platforms and not being able to operate them for more than a few months for want of adequate and comprehensive technological support. The essential technology support needed for an air force to function efficiently can only be built with a sound indigenous aviation industry base.

Technology-acceptance encompasses not only the ability to 'operate' a sophisticated system, but is a complex mix of a national scientific education base that supports and is in turn nurtured by indigenous industry. This eclectic mix has to be readily available to sustain national efforts at maintaining the necessary level of competence in sustaining air operations at the high-end of technology. The availability of any one—either national education base or indigenous industry—alone will not be sufficient to create and sustain the elaborate systems required to generate and project quality air power. One of the fundamental challenges to air forces will always remain the ability of the force to accept high-end technology and optimise its employment. Air forces that cannot build and retain this combined capacity are invariably bound to fail.

The Challenges

Towards the end of the 20th century, technology had transformed air power from being an industrial age capability to one that was embedded

---

6 Hallion, Richard P., *op cit*, p. 386.

in the information age. Technology also made air power the preferred military instrument in ensuring security through protection and projection of national interests.[7] Technology at times brought about step changes in the development of air power capabilities, necessitating positive revisions of air power doctrine. It also reemphasised the need to ensure that intellectual and professional mastery of the 'new' air power was sustained. Technology not only brought with it enormous challenges, but indicated that it also presented the opportunity to revisit some well-worn ideas and to construct new conceptual paradigms in which air power could sustain its position as a primary instrument in reinforcing the on-going political dialogue.

There are few challenges that have an enduring quality about them and therefore must be analysed in slightly more detail than others. There are also some dichotomies that come out from the interaction of technological advances and the politico-economic aspects that influence both the development and employment of air power. These are discussed in the following paragraphs.

The Cost Factor

High-end technology is not cheap, especially when the cost of research and development is factored into the overall equation. However, any air power system of calibre will need to incorporate the latest technology to perform at the necessary level. This combination of high cost and the need to have embedded leading technology in the air power systems has far reaching consequences for the efficacy of air forces. Even when high-end technologies have been made available at a relatively low financial outlay, there are other costs involved in fielding them for regular operations. In the case of aerospace technologies the combined cost could become prohibitive and may not be affordable for smaller nations with limited financial capacity. The situation is further complicated since invariably these nations will also be struggling to address the competing domestic demands for fund allocation. Even larger and more robust economies have started to baulk at the enormous capital outlay needed for aeronautical research and development and then to convert cutting edge technological developments to successful

---

7   Mason, Professor Tony, 'Rethinking the Conceptual Framework', in Gray, Peter W., (ed) *Air Power 21, Challenges for the New Century*, The Stationary Office, London, p. 236.

The Challenges of Cutting-Edge Technology

air power systems. It may be difficult to assure the adequacy of resource allocation towards cutting edge research in the future.

The question of affordability is a vexed one and should not be permitted to sway or confuse the clarity of thought required to determine the capabilities that a nation needs to ensure its fundamental security. This, however, is easier said than implemented, especially in democratic nations where conflicting interests and influences on budgetary decisions are likely to be the norm than the exception. The cost of cutting edge air power has already become prohibitively high and the situation is only going to get exacerbated into the future. This trend will always be a dampener to a democratic government's ability to adequately resource the air force, irrespective of its intentions. Trade-offs will always create a lesser than optimum solution and the capability planners will have to be cognisant of this difficult situation. Capability acquisition decisions must only be made after always answering the fundamental question—how much of the complete quantum of optimum capability can be safely shaved off to cater for the lack of resources while ensuring that the force continues to retain the minimum capability to meet the ends of national security? A difficult question of balance if ever there was one. This is however the prevailing reality, and one that will become further entrenched in the future.

Aerospace technology sits at the higher end of the technology spectrum and is correspondingly resource intensive to obtain. Therefore, it is not inconceivable that some nations, who currently possess some air power capabilities—even if they are relatively mediocre—may consider future air power to be beyond the reach of their national economies and elect to do away with it altogether. If this trend takes hold and is projected into the mid-term future it would lead to the conclusion that the overall quantum of high calibre air power available across the world will reduce in the next few decades. In this instance the term 'quantum' indicates not just air power's lethal capabilities, the point of the spear, but also the non-flashy, but critical cargo carrying airlift capabilities, that are the mainstay of most modern military forces' flexibility and responsiveness. A global decrease in military airlift capacity will have a detrimental impact on international disaster response capabilities. Reduction in the overall quantity of airlift will be an indication of the beginning of a downward turn in the efficacy of air power. It is obvious that the first factor to be analysed in a forward projection of air power and associated technologies should be the state of national economies, individually and collectively.

The cost burden of the research and developmental requirements of air power systems has reached a stage where there is a visible trend amongst the nations capable of developing such high-end technologies to invite trusted allies and partners to share the cost of research and development. The development of the Joint Strike Fighter F-35 Lightening II is a prime example of the manifestation of this trend. In the current climate of global financial austerity this trend can be expected to become established as a fully expanded 'share the cost of development if you want this technology, otherwise it will not be made available to you' attitude from the major aerospace manufacturing nations. Smaller economies with essentially limited resource availability will be forced to choose one of two options if they are to continue to maintain credible air forces: either become a dependent ally of a great power while accepting all the political implications of such a move; or accept the fact that independent air power capabilities will have to be sacrificed at the altar of an altruistic belief in national sovereignty, coupled with financial stringency. The stark reality is that smaller air forces will need dedicated government support to remain relevant within the national security equation. This situation will only become more exacerbated into the future.

A spin-off of this situation is that resources will be made available only for what is considered the bare minimum air power capability, which may not even embrace the highest levels of technology. The repercussions of such financial stringency on the performance capacity of the air force will not be felt immediately, but will only manifest over the middle- to long-term. A gradual, but certain, erosion of the overall capability of the air force is sure to take place. Further, with lesser numbers being demanded, the per item cost of an air power system will continuously increase because the numbers available to spread the research and developments costs will continue to reduce. This could lead to a vicious cycle of cost prohibiting the acquisition of greater numbers of systems that in turn increases the cost per item and so on. Some smaller air forces may not be able to contain such a vicious cycle, which would mean the inevitable decline of the overall capability and capacity of the force, leading to its eventual demise. The loss of combat capability of the Royal New Zealand Air Force a few years back is a case in point as an example of this cycle in action. However, the future is not fully gloomy. The increased effectiveness of individual systems compensates, to some degree, for the loss of overall capability and flexibility that accompany declining numbers. Even so, the increase in effectiveness and decrease in capability are not always commensurate to each other and may not be equally balanced. In this situation, overall loss of capability is an unfortunate certainty.

The increasing challenge of cost factor on air power can be illustrated by providing some statistics. In 1988, M. J. Armitage calculated the following costs in US dollars. He determined that in constant 1985 dollars, an F-100 Super Sabre fighter aircraft cost $ 2 million in 1954; an F-4 Phantom over $ 6 million in 1962; and that an F-15 Eagle cost $ 25 million in 1974. It was also assessed that in the three decades following World War II, the cost of maintaining the army grew by 2.9 per cent per annum, navy by 6.4 per cent, and the air force by 7.1 per cent.[8] Although these figures pertain specifically to the US military forces, they are irrefutable as cost trend indicators. Armitage's analysis reinforces the fact that air forces continue to be the 'costliest' to develop and sustain.

The resource-intensiveness and restricted availability of sophisticated technology brings up a further challenge to the efficacy of air power. In the future, significant air power capabilities will become resident in a lesser number of nations compared to the current situation. In the closing decades of the last century there was a prevalent belief that the technology gap between the air forces of the developed world and the so-called developing world was reducing. In the current context and well into the future, this belief has to be understood in a slightly more nuanced manner. No doubt, some of the smaller air forces will be able to acquire and operate technologically advanced air power systems. However, such situations will be few and isolated. Further, it is certain that the smaller air forces will face an uphill task in sustaining meaningful operations for any length of time, diminishing the overall effect that could be created. The efficacy of maintaining such a force itself becomes questionable. Merely possessing the latest state-of-the-

---

8 Armitage, M. J., *Unmanned Aircraft*, Potomac Publishers, Washington D.C., 1988, p. 99.

art equipment and systems does not automatically confer the status of having a coherent air power capability on a nation.

In the future, air power will have to be projected by sustainable systems comprising of technologically advanced equipment brought together by exercising sophisticated command and control processes. These systems will have to be flexibly fine-tuned and applied by professional masters of air power to create optimum effect. In other words, competent air power is an intricate play of intertwined technology, smoothened out by professional human beings. This is not easily achieved.

Mass and Technology

When applied to air power, mass must be considered to have two distinct elements in it. One is mass in terms of assets and the capabilities that an air force can bring to bear for a reasonably long duration in a given circumstance. In this regard Stalin's often quoted saying, 'quantity has a quality all its own' must be analysed. It may indeed be true that numerical superiority had a fundamental and positive influence on the outcome of any military encounter during World War II and its immediate aftermath. However, in the technologically biased contemporary air power equation, if quantity indeed must bring with it an assured statement of quality, the numbers required will be very large and probably unaffordable. Even so, there is some element of truth in the statement, especially if the warring parties are functioning at the lower end of the technology spectrum.

The second element is the mass of an air force as a single entity; the combination of its people, assets, capabilities, concepts, and every single other factor that combines to the make an effective air force. This understanding of mass reflects the fact that small and medium sized air forces normally function at 'critical mass'—the operative word in that term being 'critical', which takes away the traditional meaning of mass from this term. It also becomes clear that these air forces do not have the luxury of reliance on mass to ameliorate the demands of concurrent operations and/or the necessity to ramp up the tempo of an on-going operation at short notice. Essentially it means that an air force functioning at critical mass, has no spare capacity to cater for major and serious emergence of threats that have not been anticipated and catered for in the current campaign.

It is because this constrained situation prevails in most contemporary air forces that a clearly marked and symbiotic relationship has emerged between mass and leading edge technology. Air forces operating at critical mass will not normally have the luxury of inducting technology at the absolute cutting edge for two entwined reasons. First, cutting edge technology is something that is still in the proving stage and therefore a failure cannot be categorically ruled out. The second, and directly drawing from the first, is that small air forces operating at their critical mass will not have the ability to absorb such a failure of technology without sacrificing some amount of their capability. This loss of capability could prove strategically catastrophic if it happens at some critical phase in the employment of air power. The requirement, now and into the future, for small and medium air forces will be to stay a step behind the cutting edge in attempting to acquire/absorb/accept sophisticated technology. The need to have access to leading edge rather than cutting edge technology is emphasised in this equation.

High-end or Low-end?

Air power is expected to operate across a wide spectrum of conflict that could conceivably span multiple operations. At the lower end—where the tempo and intensity are lowest and the technological requirements are also low—the spectrum begins with the benign use of air power assets to deliver much-needed humanitarian aid and disaster relief expeditiously, and move across to the higher end when air power is employed to fight and win a war of national survival, if and when necessary. Admittedly, in the contemporary world, the probability of the occurrence of a war of national survival is minimal, although it can never be categorically ruled out. Under these circumstances, air power has to be prepared to face such an exigency, however remote it may seem. However, high-end capabilities are resource-intensive and not accessible to all nations. Therefore, the debate regarding whether an air force must maintain high-end or low-end capabilities and the appropriate force structure to do so is one without an end. This debate is particularly relevant to idle power nations in the current security environment when conventional military forces are increasingly involved in IW.

High-end air power capabilities are expensive to acquire, operate and sustain at the requisite level of expertise. Further, it takes a lengthy period of time to fully embed high-end capabilities and operate them effectively within a force. In comparison, low-end (all of them need not necessarily be low-technology) capabilities are more easily acquired and employed, while also requiring a much shorter familiarisation lead-time. Since a majority of future conflicts are likely to be conducted as IW, there are strident calls to tailor air power capabilities to fight the lower-level battles. No doubt there is merit in training and equipping for the fight at hand, but altering the force structure to cater only for an IW contingency is fraught with risk at the strategic levels of national security requirements. The cost-effective option in these circumstances will be to build an adaptable force capable of dealing with the evolving conflict situation by transitioning from one end of the spectrum to the other, in a contextual manner.

An adaptable force that can transition across the spectrum of conflict with ease invariably begets the question—should such a transition be from the high-end to the low-end or vice versa? In turn, the force structure, capability spread and primary focus of such an adaptable air force will be decided by the fundamental purpose for which the nation maintains the force. If its primary role is *not* the defence of the nation, then any kind of combination can be attempted without fear of any direct impact on the security of the nation. However, if air power is considered a relevant element within national security, the air force must have the full spread of capabilities. The question of the direction of transition in an adaptable force remains. In the case of air power, transitioning from low-end to high-end—definitely a cost-effective option—will be impossible for a number of reasons, especially considering the rapidity required to effect the changes.

The reasons can be listed: the lead-time required for a force to become proficient in the effective employment of high-end capabilities precludes their being acquired when conflict is imminent; the technological sophistication of the assets make it necessary to put in place comprehensive and long-term training regimes; air power is required to ensure adequate control of the air that in turn normally demands the employment of high-technology weapon systems; and from an air power perspective, the hardest capabilities to regenerate are the high-end ones. These major reasons automatically point to wisdom in embedding high-end capabilities that can be 'ramped down', if necessary, to meet emerging requirements. However, the debate regarding the balance between high-end and low-end capabilities will continue into the future since there can be no assured prediction of the future security needs of a nation and its domestic socio-economic situation.

Small air forces are staring at a future with limited resource availability and 'just-enough' capabilities and assets but saddled with the complete responsibility of providing credible air power options to the nation, when and where required. The flexibility and versatility to ramp up or down rapidly will be coveted characteristics and ones that must be nurtured into the future. The future air force will have to at all times maintain the right balance required to meet national security imperatives, taking into account the grand strategic objectives of the nation.

The Politics of Technology

There is a political aspect to the technology issue, which also needs elaboration. The development of high-end technology and the research necessary to convert it to effective military competencies is not only cost-intensive but also requires entrenched, long term and resident scientific expertise within the nation. None of these are easy to come by, especially the scientific tradition critical to further development of leading-edge technology through concerted research. The cost-intensiveness of high-end technology and its repercussions are straight forward and can be easily understood—either a nation has the necessary financial resources to expend on what is considered necessary technological research and development, or it does not. In the following discussion it is hypothetically assumed that sufficient funds are available for research and development in the high-end technology sector.

Since the educational base of a nation vis-à-vis technology development and acceptance has already been discussed, the other major variable of consequence is the political situation of the nation. Political developments—both domestic and global—have important parts to play in moving a nation towards scientific self-sufficiency. Domestic political debate is the fundamental input into determining the security threats to the nation, which in turn shapes the force structure and capability development requirements of its military forces. It could well be that domestic political and societal compulsions do not permit investment in high-end technology research. In this situation, an understandable and workable balance in resource allocation will have to be achieved. If this is the case, the military forces may remain competent, but may not be functioning at the leading edge of technology. International politics and the relation between nations that flow from it, and into it, are even more involved. A nation may have access to sophisticated technology purely through being formal allies with one or more greater powers. Such access will of course come with fairly stringent geo-strategic strings attached. However, smaller nations aspiring to maintain technologically sophisticated military forces may not have other options other than to accept the conditions laid down by the greater power.

The issue with acquiring high-end technology form external sources, even if the donor nation is the closest ally, is that the assurance of supply and sustenance rests with the providing nation and the recipient has almost no control over it. In other words, the situation is tantamount to indirectly bargaining with the sovereignty of the nation. The requirement therefore is for the alliance to be long-standing, mutually beneficial and built on a core of confidence between the two peoples and not purely between elected representatives. Such alliances are few and far in between. The other factor to be aware of if such a situation comes to pass is that this sort of an arrangement will invariably have a detrimental effect on the recipient nation's educational, research and scientific developmental activities. Ambitious nations, waiting at the wings for their time and place in the sun, may not be comfortable with such arrangements and would at some time or the other in their developmental saga face absolutely stark choices. The challenge is to understand the dichotomy of the options available and to make informed choices, both for the short-term and the long.

Existing Dichotomies

Technology—through its development and innovative application—today provides air power with a range of capabilities, which are exponentially better than all previous ones. Air power now is the acme of power projection capabilities. However, despite the enhanced capabilities and acceptance of its criticality to national security, the capacity of air power to create lasting strategic effects seems to have diminished. This is a dichotomy and there are six fundamental factors, which have a direct impact on the employment of air power that may, individually and in varying combinations, resolve it. Further, these factors will continue to influence the efficiency of air power well into the long-term future.

First, is the greatly enhanced, and continually increasing, speed of computation that has now clearly surpassed the ability of the human brain to keep pace with it. In a somewhat Orwellian manner, the speed of computation is now beyond human comprehension. Information, knowledge and situational awareness are critically essential to conscious decision-making. The volume of data that is required to be processed to create the necessary level of information and situational awareness is such that only computers can realistically hope to achieve the necessary decision-timeliness required for success in the modern battlespace. The result of this interface with computers has been the improved veracity of decisions, since a greater quantity of assured information is made available to the decision-maker. Even more important has been the fact that computers have shrunk the timeframe of the traditional OODA loop of decision-making to an unrecognisable fraction in comparison to earlier times. The delay, if any, in the decision-making today is that of the human brain absorbing and coming to terms with the information and knowledge that is being fed to it at an alarming rate.

If the advantages that come with the shrinking of the information-feed-timeframe are to be fully leveraged in the battlespace, then the decision-making cycle also needs to be proportionately reduced. This will invariably lead to the automation of decisions, especially at the operational level of the employment of air power. Further improvements in the effects created by air power is now likely to take place only when autonomous decisions are allowed to shorten the 'kill-chain' timeframe to a near instantaneous one.

Second, and indirectly connected to the first, is the development and gradual maturation of artificial intelligence (AI) and its impact on decision-making. The fact that battlespace success depends on the ability to function inside the OODA loop cycle of the adversary does not need reiteration. In order to achieve this in the contemporary battlespace where measured automation is taking place, it will become necessary to delineate at least some parts of the decision-making cycle to a combination of artificial intelligence and computerised knowledge production. While computers, if optimally used, provide a knowledge-edge over the adversary, it is their combination with AI that produces an instantaneous decision leading to rapid action. The trend towards achieving this situation is unmistakably visible. However, the inherent human tendency to mistrust AI is, and will continue to be, a stumbling block in fully realising this tremendous step forward.

Third, even though precision is today an accepted norm for the application of lethal air power, the combined concept of precision, proportionality and discrimination will take on a new meaning with the advent of directed energy (DE) and electronic warfare (EW) weapon systems. These weapons will alter the traditional weapon-to-target equation in a manner not seen in air warfare since the introduction of the target designator pods during the Vietnam War. DE and EW weapons will dominate the battlespace in the near future. These weapon systems bring the advantages of enhanced and assured discrimination and much greater effective ranges to the application of air power. This development could also be a counter to the proliferation of improved anti-air capabilities that have started to question the efficacy of conventional air power sensors, systems and platforms that operate below the level of leading edge technology.

When, and not if, these DE and EW weapons systems' performance reliability is improved and they become operational, the strike ranges could increase to even a 1000 kilometres. The implications are phenomenal. A number of thought provoking questions come up. These will impact directly on the conventional wisdom regarding the application of air power. What would this capability mean to the traditional concept and definitions of control of the air and air superiority? What would the accompanying changes in employment concepts mean to the current fleet of platforms that are used to ensure adequate control of the air? Projecting such capabilities forward it would seem that the so far ubiquitous air superiority fighter, the mainstay of any competent air force, will go the way of the mounted cavalry at the arrival of the machine gun and the tank. Further, if such a drastic change in system capabilities is to be fully embedded it will have to be accompanied by equally drastic force structure alterations within the force. Air forces around the world will have to undertake carefully tailored changes in all aspects of their functioning to accommodate and harness the massive upheavals in capability that are likely to be realised, even in the near-future.

Fourth, the efficacy of air power, especially when employed as a lethal force, will be a direct function of its ability to find, analyse and fix the desired target set. The neutralisation of the designated target will come only as the next step in the kill-chain. Assurance of rapid neutralisation of designated targets is already an accepted capability of air power. Therefore, finding, identifying and fixing a target assumes greater importance in the overall picture. When this concept, already coming into vogue, is moved forward to its logical conclusion it will subtly alter the understanding of the strategy of deterrence as it is envisaged today. Currently, the strategy of deterrence is based almost completely on the demonstrated will and capability of a nation to initiate offensive action when desired. With the growing importance of precision, proportionality and discrimination as the guiding principles of offensive attacks, deterrence will also depend equally on the ability of a nation to find and identify the correct centres of gravity of an adversary. Further, the ability to identify and target the centres of gravity must be demonstrated unambiguously to the potential adversary.

The failure of the strategy of deterrence when employed against irregular adversaries, harks back to the need to identify the centres of gravity. Such adversaries, mostly non-state entities, have very diffused centres of gravity which are not readily identifiable by the traditional ISR systems of air power. Only when the ISR capabilities of air power are combined with trustworthy human intelligence will the centres of gravity of irregular forces emerge clearly. The assurance of precision in air strikes and the emphasis on avoiding collateral damage has managed, in a circumspect manner, to alter the fairly simple strategy of deterrence to one that is more complex and therefore difficult to employ successfully.

Fifth, power projection is meant to dominate the battlespace, the campaign theatre and the entire area of interest in a war. However, in contemporary conflicts, dominance is moving away from being domain-dependent to an amorphous concept of multi-domain integration. Further, the cost of achieving overarching dominance, even in one domain, is becoming prohibitively high, in all areas of resource requirement—personnel, materiel, and finances. At the moment only air power is capable of domain-independent battlespace dominance. The employment of military forces, particularly air power, is now entering an era where the conventional perception and concept of dominance will alter dramatically. Power projection is moving into an epoch where dominance will be defined in a contextual manner, will be temporary and constrained in time and space. The future of dominance will be much like the current understanding and acceptance of different levels of control of the air.

In this more restrictive understanding of dominance, power projection—even within the theatre of operations—will be intimately connected to, and driven by, political objectives. Dominance as a concept moves into the strategic realm and will no longer have a purely military connotation. The definition of battlespace domination itself will have to be reinterpreted. This change in perception will automatically impinge on concept development and force structure development of an air force.

Sixth, is the use of space for military purposes and flowing from it, the placement of weapon systems in space. The dichotomy in the situation is at two different levels. The first is at the conceptual level. There are international laws and agreements in place that prohibit the use of space as a conflict area. However, it is certain that the space-capable powers would have initiated actions to move weapons into space, although there seems to be a tacit understanding that these matters will not be discussed or debated openly. There is no assurance that space will not be used for the delivery of lethal force if a powerful enough nation feels the need to do so. The dichotomy of overtly adhering to the idea of peaceful use and the covert development of the capacity to employ weapons from space is openly visible.

The second dichotomy is particularly visible in the application of air power. Air power itself has a negative cost-factor attached to it, being considered far too expensive. Even so, space-based assets continue to become increasingly important for the efficient application of air power—for both lethal and benign purposes. The prohibitive cost associated with commencing a space program and the minimum necessary technological capability needed to do so deter most nations from attempting such a venture. Obviously it is not possible for all nations to be space-capable. Therefore, space-dependency will remain the Achilles' heel of modern air forces without their own dedicated space programs of calibre, a vulnerability that can be exploited very easily by a clever adversary. The level of vulnerability increases exponentially with the advent of so-called 'rogue' nations with fledgling space capabilities. As a corollary, the ownership of space assets by the more advanced 'space nations' will remain an inherent advantage for them and their air forces. This is unlikely to change in the near future.

Conclusion

Technology—and all the various factors that are involved in understanding it—will remain a strategic challenge to air power. Air power is born of technology, nurtured by technology and totally technology-reliant to ensure its credible performance—in effect it is not an exaggeration to state that air power is built on technology. Within this paradigm, there are a number of challenges related to technology that are faced by the men and women involved in the generation and application of air power. Since the optimum performance of an air force is a direct function of technology, these challenges will need to be evaluated and ameliorated as they emerge. This is a process that will remain a constant in all calculations regarding air power into the future.

There is no doubt about and no argument against the fact that air power is a cost-intensive capability, especially when compared to surface forces. It is therefore not surprising that in a number of different nations, the same debate is brought forward by army enthusiasts that the savings accrued by reducing by a small amount the number of air power systems being purchased could be used to raise and sustain a number of battalions of infantry or to buy armour and artillery. Such arguments exhibit two facts. First, it is an open admission of an ignorance regarding the broader national security equation. Second, and more importantly, it demonstrates a lack of understanding regarding the minimum overall air power capability necessary to ensure national security and the fact that it can only be created by a minimum number of air power systems. Any shortfall in the numbers will immediately manifest as a shortfall in the holistic capability required. Such debates and statements will continue to be levelled against air power into the future and can even become emotive issues within a democracy—especially when resource allocation is central to the discussion. Air power professionals would be well-advised to be cognisant of this factor, now and into the foreseeable future.

The cost-intensiveness of air power must be explained through the prism of the demands that is placed on it by the government as well as its inherent capability to rapidly deliver strategic solutions. The greater the demand, greater will be the costs involved. The balance between cost and capability will have to be directly decided at the highest strategic level and should take into account the long-term security imperatives and posture of the nation. An overarching decision by the greater powers of the world to completely do away with air power as an instrument of military power and a force projection tool, just because it is resource-intensive and costly to acquire, maintain, employ and sustain, is not being envisaged here. In fact, if anything the reverse will be true. The inherent characteristics of air power, enhanced and honed through technological innovations, will always be a prized capability, one that nations that are serious about assuring national security and consider their intangible interests to be worth protecting, and when necessary fighting for, will nurture and develop.

The bottom line is this: yes, the cost-intensive nature of air power will always be a challenge to be overcome, especially in middle-power democracies. There can be no complete and absolute solution to this challenge since the appreciation of cost and resource implications at the national level is always relative and normally in flux. However, it must also be recognised that state-of-the-art maritime power or a capable and well-constructed army are also not cheap and cannot be acquired off-the-shelf. If this line of thought is extended to the next level, it becomes obvious that no army or navy—however technologically advanced and capable they may be and irrespective of the adversary's inferiority or superiority—will ever want to embark on a campaign without adequate assurance of control of the air. Therefore, while the challenge of technology will always have to be dealt with in the application of air power, and irrespective of the cost as well as other associated hurdles, air power will continue to be a critical element in the national security and military calculations well into the future.

Undeniably modern air power is space-dependent. The challenge for smaller air forces are two-fold: first is to ensure adequate access to space-based assets, which in turn leads to the conclusion that even without owning space-assets an air force must have an articulated space doctrine; and second, is to have a debate at the strategic level whether or not indigenous space capabilities should be developed. The implications of both are clear—space and its use cannot be ignored any more by air forces that are, or aspire to be, ones of strategic influence in the national security debate.

Increasing sophistication of aerospace technologies also mean that it now requires a longer lead-time for an air force to be able to acquire, familiarise and then operationally deploy an air power system. During times of extended peace, the reluctance of democratic governments to expend large amount of resources on military and air power capability building, will always come to the fore. The combination of these two factors detracts from a middle power air force being able to function consistently at the highest levels of technology. This is an unpalatable truth that air forces have to recognise and wear.

Chapter 4

AIR POWER SYSTEMS—INHABITED, UNINHABITED AND AUTONOMOUS

'In the future, aerospace leaders may decide to use a predominant force of UAVs in particular situations or phases of an air campaign. UAVs will alter the face of combat. Perhaps due to the absence of a pilot and any potential casualties to aircrews, national leaders will be more willing to use this form of airpower rather than surface forces. Additionally, the availability of UAVs might prompt more aggressive action rather than diplomacy.'

Clayton K.S. Chun[9]

The term 'air power system' has been consciously used in the title to this chapter since the author believes that, into the future, a single flying asset by itself will not be able to generate the quantum of quality air power that will prove to be battle-winning. There is incessant debate regarding the development and application of systems that generate air power, particularly in terms of the employment of uninhabited aerial vehicles (UAVs). The term 'unmanned' has been and continues to be used instead of 'uninhabited' for UAVs. Likewise, the newspapers and other media are prone to use the term 'drone' to indicate a remotely piloted vehicle. The correct term would be 'uninhabited' since there is always a 'human-in-the-loop' in terms of

---

9 Chun, Clayton K.S., *Aerospace Power in the Twenty-First Century: A Basic Primer*, Air University Press, Maxwell Air Force Base, Montgomery, AL, July 2001, p. 297.

the missions that these systems undertake, even though the human is not physically located within the body of the vehicle. This human-in-the-loop situation may not involve the actual piloting of the vehicle but could only be exercising command and control of the mission.

More importantly, the decision to launch a lethal weapon is always taken by a human being within the mission-control cycle. While current technology is already capable of applying complete autonomy in carrying out a mission, so far the application of lethal force has not been an autonomous function of these systems. Even if complete autonomy is granted in the future to specific missions, there will invariably be a 'veto' system in place that could be activated by the overseeing human-in-the-loop. While these platforms are 'uninhabited', they are controlled remotely by human operators. This situation is unlikely to change in the near-term future. Therefore, the distinct advantage that UAVs bring is not a sort of 'fire and forget' solution to the application of air power, but the fact that by employing UAVs it can be ensured that one's own airmen are kept out of harm's way when required in a conflict.

Autonomous systems have already become a reality in civil society and their employment will only increase with improving technological sophistication. Simultaneously, their utility in the battlefield has already been proven and again, the employment envelope will only increase with time. However, technological developments that tend to increase the employment of autonomous systems bring to the fore some irrefutable facts and questions. Will inhabited aircraft become redundant in the near future? Will uninhabited combat aerial vehicles (UCAVs) become the mainstay of the strike elements within the air forces? Will air power be applied by a mix of both, and if so, what will be the balance? Will true autonomy facilitated through artificial intelligence (AI) be embraced by air power? Essentially the fundamental question remains, what will be the role of lethal autonomous systems in the future? The questions are numerous, and the on-going debate is endless.

Irrespective of the legal position and the ethical debate, there is no doubt that UAVs are here to stay and that they will be increasingly preferred by military forces to carry out the more dangerous missions, the ones that are referred to as the first-day of war missions. They will also be the preferred option for the 'dull' missions, which require loitering over the area of interest endlessly, even beyond human endurance limits, in order to gather intelligence. Primarily because of these two employment concepts, UAVs are assuming increasingly greater importance in the overall air power picture. The ubiquitous nature of UAVs have now seen them being used very successfully in many different roles. They are now routinely used for intelligence, surveillance and reconnaissance (ISR), provision of time-sensitive lethal strikes, and even in counter-IED (improvised explosive devices) missions. However, there is a growing number of questions being asked regarding the employment of UCAVs to carry out targeted strikes, especially regarding the ethics and morality of such actions. This becomes further vexed when the legal status of such operations are at times considered to be in the grey zone within the currently accepted laws of armed conflict.

Intelligence, Surveillance and Reconnaissance

The use of UAVs with long endurance and flying at high-altitudes, the altitude providing a sort of protection to these defenceless and relatively slow platforms, for gathering data through persistent monitoring of areas of interest has now been accepted as being the optimum way to conduct ISR. However, there is one fundamental misconception regarding this UAV role that must be dispelled. It is generally believed that a high-latitude, long-endurance (HALE) UAVs will be able to stay on station almost indefinitely and monitor the actions of the potential target without being visible or intrusive. To a certain extent this is true.

What is not common knowledge is that the current crop of UAVs have a limited geographic 'view' and cannot be used for 'broad area' surveillance. Therefore they need the required area of surveillance to be initially delineated to a manageable size. This is achieved through the employment of manned[10] surveillance aircraft that have the ability to view large areas and identify the areas of interest in a more geographically limited manner, which is then passed to the UAV for long-term surveillance. The other factor to note is that their relatively

---

10 Here the term 'manned' is not meant in a gender-specific manner, but only denotes that the platform is inhabited by a human being who is/are the operators of the airborne system.

slow speed of transit from one area to another, limits their flexibility to be used in different areas of interest at will. A large theatre cannot be effectively covered by UAVs unless they are available in large numbers. Cost-effectiveness, which is one of the advantages of employing UAVs, is lost in this situation. Air power still relies heavily on manned surveillance platforms to carryout ISR in a more responsive manner and to cover larger swaths of area. This is particularly applicable to maritime surveillance missions. The fact is that UAVs are not the panacea to all challenges of ISR, at least for the time being.

Even in the future, the limitations of slow speed and constraints of the area that can be covered will continue to inhibit the ISR capabilities of UAVs. The technology to make them faster does exist, but if such technologies are incorporated into the UAVs, it will have to be at the cost of the UAVs becoming more expensive and thereby losing the appeal that they have of being resource-saving systems. Further, if the surveillance equipment is made more sophisticated to improve its performance, two reactive developments will take place. The size of the platform will increase to cater for a higher payload that in turn will lead to a requirement for larger engines and more fuel, further increasing the actual size. This will lead to a vicious cycle that will be a self-defeating process, as the primary advantage of cost-effectiveness would have been jettisoned on the wayside in perpetuating this process. From an ISR perspective, it would seem that well into the future, UAVs will remain with similar capabilities to what they have now, may be with some minor improvements.

Uninhabited Combat Aerial Vehicles

Employing armed UAVs, now termed UCAVs, to deliver lethal strikes is a great concept, especially when considered for the 'dull and dirty' missions that carry a higher level of risk for aircrew. It has already been clearly demonstrated that UCAVs can provide rapid, on-call precision strike capability. However, the utilisation of UCAVs as an instrument of military power is a vexed topic with the arguments for and against their use ranging in a very large spectrum for many years now. The debate raises a number of questions. There are a few unresolved issues that will keep coming up continually in all discussions regarding the use of UAVs, and more importantly in the employment of UCAVs. Even so, the employment of UCAVs is becoming increasingly common among the premier air forces of the world.

The first issue that will inhibit their unrestricted use is the cost factor involved in increasing the sophistication of UCAVs. Their increasing popularity in military usage is based on two characteristics; first, they are cheap and therefore, in a purely resource calculation matrix, relatively more expendable; and second, they avoid placing human beings at extreme risk during dangerous operations. The initial success of these systems automatically placed greater demands on them and technology obliged. Today, technology provides U(C)AVs with the ability to stay on station for days at a time, provide live feed of its surveillance results to remote locations half-way round the world, and the capability to carry lethal precision weapons that can be remotely targeted and released.

The concept has been proven to be successful in battle zones, especially where the airspace is not contested and relatively benign. However, it is also seen that UCAVs require greater operating speeds to enhance survivability and also improve responsiveness. This demand in turn forces the design developmental need to cater for larger platforms to house bigger engines and also carry more fuel and larger weapon payload. These improvements have greatly increased the price tag of these machines, thereby neutralising their fundamental advantage of being expendable. When survivability is also dependent on the incorporation of stealth and other self-defence mechanisms, the cost and the complexity of operations are increased exponentially. Considering that the initial ubiquitous nature of UCAVs in air power operations was based on their cost-effectiveness, the challenge now is to balance the cost-escalation that comes with enhanced capability. How much capability gain can be made while continuing to have the UCAVs considered to be throw-away systems is not an easy question to answer. The challenge will continue to be one that air power strategists will have to grapple with into the future, perhaps with no acceptable answer to it. The future debates regarding the efficacy of UCAVs will invariably centre on this factor.

The second issue is the question of asset requirement to carry out strikes on time-sensitive and fleeting targets of opportunity. Mostly such targets will be the leadership of irregular forces, essentially human targets. In order to be successful in a strike against a human target with the assurance of minimal collateral damage, the asset requirement—in terms of the extended periods of surveillance required and the availability of the attack UCAV's 'on-call'—will be very high. Even when the surveillance platform itself carries the weapon, the success rate probability of such missions does not alter significantly. When the necessity to first locate and then track the target through extensive ISR is added to the mission profile, this process may not prove to be the most efficient, both operationally and in terms of resource utilisation. The other side of the coin is that the large asset requirement for successful conduct of such missions that combine the ISR and strike processes makes it viable and sustainable only for large air forces that have sufficiency in assets.

The third issue that has not been fully addressed is the question of the legal status of UCAV operators within the Laws of Armed Conflict (LOAC). Currently their status remains vague even after more than a decade of their operations and the trend towards dramatically increasing their employment as seen in the past few years. The situation is complicated by the fact that a number of these operators are civilians who do not come under the ambit of the LOAC, at least for now. They are therefore not 'covered' under the Geneva Convention and other protocols that protect the rights of soldiers. The current state of the world does not provide any hope for a general consensus to be arrived at in this dilemma. It is certain that the human operators of UCAVs will continue to be in legal limbo well into the future. Even so, the employment of UCAVs by the larger powers is unlikely to be curtailed, in fact it is only likely to increase.

The fourth issue is the question of survivability of the UCAVs, especially when they have gone beyond being expendable purely from a resource expenditure and requirement calculation. The 'arm-chair strategists and warriors' have proclaimed UCAVs as the answer to the controversial question of attrition tolerance and the need to balance the application of lethal force from the air with minimal risk to own forces. This opinion is based on a narrow focus on the efficacy of UCAVs in a benign air environment and does not take into account the diverse operating environments, adversary capabilities, and the political circumstances under which a particular air campaign will be conducted.

UCAVs have been extensively and successfully used in Afghanistan over the past decade and more. Their relative success, which has been almost completely because of the permissive airspace over the theatre, has created a wrong perception of their ubiquity and more so their survivability. During the Soviet invasion, 1979-89, the Afghan Mujahedeen had been supplied with the Stinger man-portable air defence systems (MANPADS) by the US through its allies, which made Soviet air operations by helicopter gunships and fighter jets difficult to sustain. A mere extrapolation of this situation will clearly demonstrate that UCAVs, which are relatively slower and less manoeuvrable than either helicopters or fighter jets, are not viable operational assets in air spaces whose control is contested even nominally.

The question of survivability, when combined with the non-expendable status of most UCAVs, makes them unviable for employment in contested air spaces. In these circumstances, air power will have to revert to manned assets and systems that have self-protection/-defence capabilities. The UCAVs will also have to retain the flexibility of having a 'human-in-the-loop' at the forward end of the decision-making node. Total autonomous operations will continue to be a chimera in the far future. At least for the near future, UCAVs while being useful and at times crucial assets, will continue to be only a contributory capability to the broader combat air power capability. They are highly unlikely to step over the threshold to become the mainstay of a war-winning strategy, concepts of operation or primary tactics. However, as a corollary, it is also necessary to ensure that the development of any new concept of operations for the employment of air power should incorporate the crucial role that UCAVs will play in future air campaigns.

The Western military forces have been involved in irregular wars for more than 15 years now, and the situation is unlikely to change in the near-term future. It will be prudent for capable air forces around the world to analyse the campaigns that have so far been conducted to find answers to two basic questions. One, will the conventional military forces of the world be fighting irregular campaigns with similar characteristics into the foreseeable future? And two, what role will a UAV and/or a UCAV play in a future campaign whose characteristics are not similar but incorporate some other dimensions, especially if it is conducted against adversaries with some air power capabilities, even if they are minimal?

The answers to these two questions will determine the future developmental thrust of UCAVs. Currently the focus of development shows a trend towards furthering the use of artificial intelligence (AI) in these vehicles, to make them more autonomous. Deeper analysis shows this focus to be a clear case of misplaced priorities. The technological research and development should instead be focused on improving UCAV survivability in a contested airspace. The basic question of survivability could become the proverbial Achilles' heel of the entire spread of uninhabited aerial vehicles or systems, especially as the cost per unit continues to mount.

UAVs and UCAVs are 'good to have' assets rather than 'must have' assets, especially for smaller air forces. In the contemporary political scenario in democratic nations, where resources are limited and stringently controlled, the perception of military needs is always influenced with populist measures that require to be adopted to influence the domestic voting public. In such conditions, it needs a visionary approach to ensure that the 'uninhabited' capability is correctly balanced vis-à-vis other air power systems. The conflicts of the immediate past, and the one's that the liberal democratic nations are currently involved in do not provide a tired and tested blue-print for the future. At the risk of sounding assuredly predictive, it can be stated that Western nations are highly unlikely to get sucked into a land-centric fight against irregular adversaries in the future. In this scenario, uninhabited aerial capabilities would be a handy tool to have in the arsenal.

Unfortunately the proponents of uninhabited systems tend to emphasise their operational advantages without contextualising their employment or the risks that are inherent in their utilisation in unfavourable conditions. There is no doubt that the uninhabited vehicles have a niche role in the capability spectrum of an air force. It has also been demonstrated that they provide an asymmetry of their own when employed under optimum conditions. However, it is highly likely that for the foreseeable future, 'niche' is what they will remain, without becoming a substitute for the broader competencies that a high-end capable air force brings to bear in a conflict.

Artificial Intelligence and Autonomy

Into the contentious debate regarding the employment of UCAVs, the question of the use of AI has been introduced. Dependent on firmly held opinions of the protagonists, the discussion becomes acrimonious and borders on the vicious. Futuristic concepts of operations and emerging employment opportunities point towards the benefits of blending AI with UCAVs to make them into a single combined capability. However, at least for the near-term a pragmatic assessment of their future utility needs to consider them separately. From an air power perspective it is necessary to analyse and understand the individual traits, nuances and intricacies of employing each of them before the practicalities of combining the two can be explored.

AI is the 'intelligence' that is inserted into a 'robot'—the term 'robot' being used here to denote any machine capable of perambulation on its own and not in a domain-centric manner—to ensure that it functions in an autonomous manner without any human input for the full span of an independent mission. Technologically, this is already feasible. From a purely scientific point of view, the development of AI has reached a stage wherein it is very close to becoming a human-like capability. In fact, the combination of uninhabited vehicles and AI have proven to be extremely successful in terms of the machine carrying out mundane and specific jobs. Even so, when it comes to using this combination for the application of lethal force, the situation is altered in a discernible manner. The UCAV-AI combination has still not reached a stage of maturity where the human commanders are likely to trust them implicitly. This lack of trust is based on a number of factors, which primarily include the fear of failure and the enormous political consequences of it. The onus of responsibility of having made a 'wrong' decision through letting the artificial intelligence take charge of the mission is far too high in political terms. Currently no military force or nation employs fully autonomous lethal systems—airborne or on the surface—a situation that is unlikely to change soon.

The inherent human tendency to resist change; the apprehension of not being in 'control', which in itself brings out a sense of inadequacy;

and the sub-conscious need to maintain human supremacy in a man(human)-machine interface are also significant influences that inhibit the possible employment of AI in a more meaningful manner. While the psyche of distrust of individualistic machines has been built into the human being over generations, it will take even longer to gradually convert this distrust to belief. Once unfettered trust has been built-in, it can be converted to the uninhibited employment of AI under all circumstances. This radical change in perception will need concerted education of the decision-makers to achieve the necessary acceptance. More importantly, acceptance would also need to come from the lay person, who would otherwise question the wisdom of letting machines make decisions that deal with life and death of human beings. When the human is completely removed from the loop in the decision-making cycle regarding the application of lethal force that is intended to kill and destroy, the fundamental doctrine and leadership ethos of a military force, as it exists today, will be the first to be questioned and made redundant. Unfortunately, in the absence of any existing foundation to base the developments of new theories, the risk of an explosion of anarchical concepts is both real and worrisome.

Stemming from the purely cognitive human element of trust and distrust, there is a visible political reluctance to give complete freedom of action to fully-automated combat vehicles. This is particularly so when the mission is to engage the adversary with the application of lethal force, fully at the discretion of the machine-AI combination. There is another background influence to this visible reluctance. Over the past few decades, collateral damage in the application of lethal military force has become increasingly unacceptable at the political level. Popular opinion, fanned by frenetic media reporting has created completely negative connotations of collateral damage from a humanitarian viewpoint. Further, when such unintended damage is caused as a result of the employment of air power, for some inexplicable reason, the condemnation of the air force and the nation involved is the most vociferous. There is invariably a frenzy of press coverage. The fact that in all kinds of military operations, even in situations in which the decision to apply lethal force was made by a human being on the spot in a considered manner, there can never be complete assurance of avoiding collateral damage goes unnoticed and unreported. In such a scenario, collateral damage created by a UCAV-

AI combination will never be politically acceptable. Closing this circle of argument, it can be stated with certainty that the end result will be that fully autonomous application of lethal air power, a judicious combination of a UCAV and AI, is unlikely to become a reality in the near future.

Another factor that is often overlooked in this intangible sphere of distrust and belief is the role played by popular cinema and science fiction literature that often portray scary versions of 'robots' running wild in an effort to 'rule' the humans. This has influenced the public perception and created a belief against autonomous vehicles, undermining the limited support for the optimised employment of UCAVs or other robots. The other issues that inhibit the unrestricted use of UCAVs pale into insignificance when the use of AI to give complete autonomy to UCAVs is considered.

For all kinds of reasons, both major and minor, AI will not be considered fully 'reliable' and will not be completely 'trusted' at least in the near future. Even if AI demonstrates its reliability for years, a single mistake would bring it back to the starting line where the trust will have to be built all over again. There is, and probably will always be, reluctance within the strategic leadership and decision-making bodies, particularly at the political level, to leave the final decision to carry out a lethal strike entirely to AI without human oversight and veto. This means that complete autonomy for lethal systems is not on the horizon as yet, although the direction of air power growth clearly indicates a trajectory towards increased usage of AI. The best scenario that can be achieved in the mid-term future is for the UCAV-AI combined system to function with a deliberate human veto capability built into it—a sort of a hybrid where the human-in-the-loop through the entire mission cycle is removed and replaced by a human peeping over the shoulder of AI only at the critical decision points of weapon release.

The progress of enhanced usage of AI is also bogged down in the swirling debate regarding the moral, ethical and legal aspects attached to it. AI itself is an emotive issue in many quarters, which detracts from a pragmatic debate regarding its usefulness. This in turn produces a less than optimum approach to its realistic and considered employment. The situation has been exacerbated by the fact that the actual development of AI has not kept pace with the promises that scientists have made regarding its potential and efficacy. There is a sense that AI development has hit a plateau for some time now—whether it is through benign neglect because of the lack of use or through a genuine lack of scientific breakthrough is unclear. AI is a futuristic capability and will find its niche in the future, although it is difficult to predict the timeframe of this happening with any assurance. Its usage will continue to be within 'human-in-the-loop' operations for the foreseeable future.

There is a school of thought that AI will in the very near future be advanced to an extent that missions could be conducted successfully without a human within the decision cycle—at least at the operational and tactical levels of war. This is the dream of robotics scientists. Indeed there is no doubt that AI capable of making weapon release decisions will be fielded, sooner rather than later; they could well be already in the trial mode. However, there is a counter assertion to be made to this progress. The author firmly believes, and he is not alone in this belief, that decisions that would result in the death of human being(s)—irrespective of their affiliation, status as adversaries etc.,—cannot, and should not, unilaterally be made by AI-infused machines. The practical options that emerge during the actual aerial combat phase of an operation will eventually prove to be too complex for AI to comprehensively handle, even if it has been programmed to respect international law. Therefore, while AI will be used to facilitate the operations of UAVs and UCAVs, it is certain that there will always be a human in the decision-making cycle, even if the human only has a veto call, when the lethal application of force is being contemplated.

The unrestricted employment of UCAV-AI combine is hindered by another challenge. Currently there is no facility to fully integrate autonomous UCAVs into the broader structure, at the strategic level of command and control of a campaign. The farthest the conceptual structure has been considered is for an inhabited platform—a fighter or an airborne early warning and control aircraft to act as a sort of mother-ship—to control a number of UCAVs, which could be then employed as required by the human in overall command. Even such a scenario is currently only a concept and far from reaching even the experimentation stage; it remains a far-fetched dream. The idea requires a great deal more of refinement and both operational and tactical interpretation before it can be considered for trial as a concept of operation. Considering the impediments, this may be many decades away.

If and when both the political and military strategic leadership accept the efficacy of letting UCAVs operate in a fully autonomous mode in conjunction with AI, there will be visible and long-lasting changes that take place in the battlespace vis-à-vis the ways to achieve strategic objectives. These will be, of necessity, accompanied by revision of concepts of operations and development of altered tactical appreciation. A number of questions will emerge and they need to be answered satisfactorily if the UCAV-AI combination is to become fully operational. Is there a role for the human in this combine other than at the very beginning of a mission? Should a built-in monitoring system with an infallible veto be incorporated in the cycle for the foreseeable future? How will UCAV-AI combine affect the philosophical level doctrine and strategy of air power? Will the essential changes in strategy percolate to make changes necessary in the force structure and capability development?

The evolution of the UCAV-AI employment theories are reminiscent of the thinking process regarding aircraft during the inter-war years, 1918-39. All the theories and ideas were based on conjuncture, buttressed by some wishful thinking. This was unavoidable since there was no explicit experience to base the development of these theories and concepts. Answering the emerging questions regarding the UCAV-AI combination and maturing the developmental concepts will take time and will be strewn with mistakes. There is no other way to chart a course into an unknown future.

From the employment perspective of air power, where does this leave the UCAV-AI combination, which must be considered the foundation for future autonomous operations? The very obvious advantage of the UCAV-AI combination is that it can create a 'launch-and-forget' capability for the application of lethal force from the air. It is also not inconceivable that such a vehicle could be programmed to 'hide' while functioning in the surveillance mode, becoming visible only during the terminal phase of target designation and neutralisation, when used in the strike role. This scenario would be the ultimate dream come true for air power advocates and will enhance the strike capabilities of air power, especially when pitted against targets of fleeting opportunity. However, even this tailor-made scenario will have to be understood within the ambit of few caveats—it can only happen in a benign airspace where there is no air opposition, or the airspace has been carefully sanitised through a concerted air superiority campaign; and the intelligence that delineated the surveillance area is accurate enough to ensure that the chances of collateral damage are negligible.

The necessity to have adequate control of the air for autonomous or other uninhabited aerial vehicles to operate effectively in the strike and ISR roles brings to the fore yet another challenge to the UCAV-AI combination—their utility in the air superiority campaign and their future employment in a dedicated air combat role. At least for the medium-term it is highly unlikely that an autonomous or even a semi-autonomous UCAV will be employed within the broad spectrum of air superiority missions. In the extremely complex mission profiles that constitute an air superiority campaign, free-ranging operations of UCAVs would only be an impediment, at least within the current construct of command and control and concepts of operation. Far reaching changes in the command and control infrastructure from the strategic to the tactical level will have to be instituted before considering changes to concepts of operations in the campaign to achieve air superiority. In the absence of the UCAV-AI combine achieving the necessary maturity, the air superiority campaign is unlikely to see such momentous changes in the near to mid-term future.

Air power has definitely taken the first steps towards employing autonomous platforms in missions that are considered to be high-risk for the aircrew concerned—normally against critical fixed and/or mobile ground targets such as air defence systems. It is envisaged that further progress will not be as breathtaking as it has so far been, rather it will be, of necessity, slow, spasmodic and even pedantic. However, the number of manned platforms that are used in the offensive strike role will reduce by a certain amount, while remaining the mainstay of the strategic strike calculation for the foreseeable future. They may also be gradually eased into the role of 'mother-ships' to control UCAVs in their operational missions. The 'human-in-the-loop' will continue to need a broad view of the battlespace rather than a limited tunnel vision. The mother-ship concept also comes with a caveat that such control would initially be exercised at the lowest tactical level, dedicated to the neutralisation of one single pre-selected target with extremely limited flexibility to switch roles or change targets. The inherent flexibility of air power, a cornerstone of its efficacy, resides in strategic level control that needs a clear understanding and picture of the broad theatre of operations.

UCAVs have become a ubiquitous part of the battlefield and will further entrench their role as their capabilities improve and mature. However, for the foreseeable future they will continue to play their current role—carrying out strikes on fleeting targets of opportunity, located generically through intelligence and identified by limited area, long duration surveillance conducted by armed UAVs. This entire mission will have to be planned within a benign or sanitised airspace. The futurists who predict a battlespace inhabited only by autonomous vehicles—both on the surface and in the air—are dealing in the realm of science fiction. Air forces will have to wait for some more decades before such a scenario could be even trialled.

Ethical Considerations

Air attacks during war or conflict kill and maim human beings, most of the time in a focused manner. This is the hard reality of war. However, the soldier, sailor or airman who decide to and then use lethal force in the battlefield, even if the decision is near-instantaneous, is sub-consciously cognisant of the effects the taking of a life would have in terms of the future influence on the local population, the possibility of creating more enemies etc. A UCAV-AI combined system, however evolved, will not have the ability to consider these aspects. This remains the fundamental difference between having and not having a human-in-the-loop, even with only a remote veto.

The other side of the coin is that autonomous systems ensure that one's own military personnel are not at risk of injury or death and also that the onus of responsibility in making the decision to apply lethal force is removed to a degree. In an indirect manner this would make the decision to 'go to war' much easier to make, which could lead to an increase in the circumstances of the employment of military forces. When only one's own human cost is calculated and it seems to be negligible, it would seem extremely simple to order targeted assassinations with impunity. The decisions to carryout 'drone strikes' in Pakistan and the Horn of Africa were taken without much debate since the lives of US servicemen were never at risk in those operations. The ethical quandary and bankruptcy of such decisions is very seldom debated.

An error-free war can only exist as a myth. However, there is a necessity to create an ethically acceptable legal framework within which fully autonomous systems could be employed. Considering the absence of the essentially human trait of empathy and emotion, this would restrict the use of the UCAV-AI combination to a very limited spectrum. There are still a number of questions that cannot be conclusively answered with regard to the employment of fully automated lethal systems. Can an autonomous system evaluate proportionality correctly? Is it possible for an autonomous system to calculate second and third order effects of the actions that it is initiating? At the absolute bottom line who bears the responsibility for a wrong decision made by the system? Is it possible to create a legal system that comprehensively attributes responsibility for the actions of an autonomous system? Unless these and other equally complex questions can be answered, the use of such systems will never become a reality.

Conclusion

The Western nations have now been at 'war' continuously for more than two decades. In all the campaigns that have been mounted during this period, air power has undeniably been a critical factor, as both the supported and the supporting element. While the sharp end of the spear—the combat capabilities resident in the fighter fleets of air forces—continue to be employed on an as required basis, the efficacy of the employment of Uninhabited Aerial Systems[11] (UAS) have also increased to an extent where in some cases they have become the primary air power systems. They have proven to be prized assets to provide much needed ISR as well as to effect time-sensitive strikes on fleeting targets. There is no doubt that they have proven to be effective and successful in both these roles. Their visible success has however

---

11 The term UAS is being used in the conclusion to encompass both UAVs and UCAVs, as well as other more sophisticated systems that are uninhabited, but have a human-in-the-loop during its operations.

had an unanticipated effect of somewhat skewing the perception and understanding of air power in the public domain. The fact that UAS can only be used in uncontested airspaces has been lost sight of in the repeated successes of their employment, gradually bringing in a perception of air power being an infallible power projection capability that does not endanger one's own personnel. This a fallacy.

The UAS industry continues to witness significant technological developments and the systems themselves are enjoying widespread proliferation in their employment globally. An increasing number of air forces are adopting these systems into their concepts of operation and acquiring these assets into their order of battle, primarily because of their expanding spectrum of capabilities. The UAS have now been re-roled for humanitarian aid and disaster relief (HADR) missions and also to monitor the migration patterns of thousands of refugees flowing into Europe from the Middle East and North Africa. Side-by-side to these developments, counter-UAS technologies are also being developed in response to the threat being posed by UAVs operated by terrorist organisations and capable of delivering airborne improvised explosive devices.

Although UAS have proven their worth when employed in a benign airspace, their vulnerability to even a low calibre air defence system ensures that a credible air force will need to have both inhabited and uninhabited assets in a balanced mix to be effective. This balance within the force will reflect the role of the air force as envisaged within the nation' security calculus. At the operational level this mix would be contextual and vary according to the campaign and the missions being envisaged for the force. The definitive fact remains that UAS have become an indelible sub-set of the broader air power assets that a credible air force will field. While UAVs and UCAVs will not completely supplant inhabited platforms and systems well into the future, their employment will only increase as technology provides answers to the issues and challenges that currently constrain their uninhibited use in conflict situations.

Chapter 5

AIR FORCE: FUTURE FOCAL POINTS

'An air force is always verging on obsolescence and, in times of peace, its size and replacement rate will always be inadequate to meet the full demands of war. Military air power should, therefore, be measured to a large extent by the ability of the existing air force to absorb in time of emergency the increase required by war together with new ideas and techniques.'

General Henry H. Arnold[12]

The air force of a nation is the primary repository of national air power. In order to optimally leverage the inherent and unique characteristics of air power, successful air forces have become intrinsically dynamic organisations, agile in their approach to projecting power in the pursuit of national security. Adopting such an agile approach to air power employment is critical to ensure its success. Only the inherent flexibility of the air force will permit it to fully utilise the continuous enhancements taking place in air power capability, brought about through technological innovation and sophisticated conceptual developments. Dynamism has always been the hallmark of air forces. While it can normally be considered an evolutionary

---

12 Arnold, General Henry H., Exert from the Third Report to the Secretary of War, as Commanding General of the Army Air Forces of the United States of America, as published in 'Air Power and the Future', in Eugene M. Emme (ed), *The Impact of Air Power: National Security and World Politics*, D. Van Nostrand Company Inc., Princeton, New Jersey, 1959, p. 305.

process, air forces of calibre tend to consciously develop agility[13] in a focused manner. Dynamism is relatively intangible and is the capacity or trait that revolutionises the application of air power. This is a rather categorical statement and needs expansion and explanation.

The dynamism of a force is built on its ability to identify and focus on the development of the necessary personnel, organisational and conceptual requirements that together will ensure the adaptability and flexibility of the force as a whole. There are four focal points in an air force that are critically important to its well-being and cannot be lost sight of without detriment to the force. The future developmental trends in these four areas will have a salutary effect on the application of air power and therefore will affect capability development and force structure design of the force. The four focal points, in no order of priority are: Concepts, Capabilities, People, and Organisation.

Concepts

The national security strategy is derived from the Grand Strategy of a nation. It is supported by a hierarchy of concepts, which build from a broad base at the tactical level and provide the broad framework for the more focused ones that finally reach the national level. The concepts can also be considered to be cascading groups that emanate from the strategic to the ones that support the tactical application of air power. The military forces have an overarching strategy for its employment that is well-aligned with the national security strategy. This strategy is the fountainhead which in turn provides the guidelines for the development of subsidiary concepts that steer the actual employment of capabilities. Normally these are called the concepts of operations.

A higher level concept of operation functions at the lower strategic levels and can at times dip down into the higher reaches of the operational level. The veracity of such a concept of operation is important not only for the success of the application of air power, but also for the individual application of all elements of national power. Each element should therefore have an independent concept of operation. These concepts should align well with the concepts of other elements and

---

13 Dynamism and agility are essentially not the same, although they complement each other when present in the same organisation. Dynamism: the force or active principle on which a thing, person, or movement operates. Agile: quick and light in movement.

should also be directly linked to the senior concept, which should form the common foundation. Ideally there should exist a clearly defined hierarchy of concepts that, when taken together, is aligned with each other and focused on achieving national security imperatives.

Ensuring that the concept development process is absolutely correct is far more critical for the military forces than other elements of national power. This is so because putting a wrongly calculated concept into practice in the application of lethal force will have disastrous consequences, invariably involving the loss of life. In the case of other elements of national power the results of miscalculations and failures are relatively easier to control through the incorporation of corrective measures even while the process of application is in progress. By virtue of the consequences of its actions, a military force does not have this luxury and therefore cannot be sanguine about concept development. The high probability of loss of life if an inadequate concept is developed and practised is the fundamental reason for concepts of operations being of primary importance to military forces.

If there is one constant in the development of air power efficacy in the past one hundred years of its existence, it is the fact that the concepts that underpin its application have been continually changing. This has come about because of the developments in technology that have ranged from slow evolution to exponential growth. The concept development process for the application of air power has moved so rapidly forward and today epitomises the coming together of technology and human intellect. Concepts that were considered appropriate even a few decades ago have become redundant. At times some of them are even viewed with apprehension as to how such a concept was allowed to be developed, let alone effectively fielded. The idea of area bombing in World War II—carried out with absolutely no qualms or considerations regarding the collateral damage and civilian casualties that was inflicted, just because it was thought necessary in the all-out effort to win the war—is one such. Today the concept of area bombing is considered not only completely unacceptable but also deplorable in hindsight. Concept development in the application of air power has successfully enveloped the technological innovations that permit the conduct of aerial attacks with pinpoint accuracy, even from uninhabited airborne platforms.

A concept of operation that delivered astonishingly successful results in one particular conflict may not produce the same result or even be effective in a contextually different campaign. The one certainty in the on-going evolution of an air force is the fact that yesterday's and today's concepts will almost always fail to have a one hundred percent effectiveness when applied in tomorrow's campaign. This unchanging paradigm makes it imperative for air forces to retain, at all costs, the ability to innovate and develop transitory concepts 'on-the-go', trusting the steadfastness of their innate flexibility. Irrespective of the sophistication of the systems that an air force operates, flexibility and adaptability in their employment born of the agile thinking of professional airmen—overarching strategic and operational agility—will be the cornerstone on which its successes are built. Concepts of operations form an indelible part of this equation and the versatility of the concept development process contributes directly to making an air force truly agile. Air power has always met emerging challenges through leveraging its flexibility, and it will continue to do so into the future.

In the case of air power and air forces, sophisticated and viable concepts lead the way to ensure their effectiveness. Developing such concepts—at the strategic and operational levels—is a direct function of the professional mastery of the force. The high technology base required for air forces to be operationally effective brings with it the challenge of having to follow a slightly different concept development process than would otherwise have been the case. Of necessity, the process will have to be two-pronged. On the one hand the emerging technologies and the capabilities that they bring will have to be carefully analysed while on the other, practical concepts of operations for the application of force will have to be generated simultaneously. The emerging capabilities would have to be assessed within the ambit of national security requirements and thereafter superimposed on the optimised concepts of operations. This stage of the development process is fraught with the real risk of it going wrong, since it is a futuristic process with no past precedents to go by and no historical examples to emulate.

In these conditions, professional mastery of the force as a whole, and individually of the personnel involved, will be the only mechanism available that will have the capacity to mitigate any false starts. Further, professional mastery will ultimately have to take the responsibility to steer the application of air power in the right direction. The process of mitigation is relatively easier when the changes taking place are evolutionary rather than revolutionary. This means that the inherent dynamism of air power, the ability to anticipate and adapt is better served by instituting evolutionary changes even if they are unanticipated. Future concept development processes will need to be cognisant of this factor, but must also take into account the possibility of a Black Swan event that could completely neutralise, what was till then a viable concept, rapidly. This aspect will also be influenced by the fact that although the air domain is an independent entity, it influences and is in turn influenced by the other domains—land, maritime, space and cyberspace—both directly and indirectly.

A classic example of evolving concepts leading to success was demonstrated during Operation Unified Protector, the NATO air campaign in Libya conducted between March and October 2011. In this case, air power enforced a strategy of coercion on recalcitrant adversaries and was pivotal in removing an oppressive dictator from power. During the campaign, air power was able to continually evolve the concepts of operation in line with changing priorities and objectives to be achieved. In providing this example of the evolutionary nature of concepts, the political aspects of the intervention and whether or not NATO exceeded the UN mandate is not being discussed, since those considerations are beyond a pure analysis of the air campaign.

The success of future concepts, and the veracity of their development process, can only be ensured by the concepts being formulated by professional masters of the air domain and through the adoption of a modulated approach that is capable of withstanding the vagaries and complexities of war. As air power capabilities become further enhanced and its application become further constrained because of extraneous reasons, development of viable concepts will become a complicated exercise. It will be a visionary air force that puts in place the foundations for such development today so that it is not found wanting tomorrow.

Capabilities

Air power capabilities that create the competence to control the air, neutralise targets effectively, move things through the air and create situational awareness have been the basis for its ascendancy in the broader arena of military capabilities. Under normal circumstances, the currently resident capabilities of an air force drive concept development. This means that concepts are developed in such a manner to ensure that the available capabilities will be able to practically employ the concept in an optimum manner. It is posited here that a majority of air forces today have been forced to adopt the sequence of cutting the coat (concept) according to the available cloth (capabilities). This makes abundant sense in a world driven by resource constraints. Even though the process is not ideal, and could even be considered slightly lopsided, it strikes a balance for the here and now. After all developing a fancy concept that cannot be supported or put into operation by the extant capabilities of the force will only make the air force remain a paper tiger. This is a fundamental truth.

Even so, in the future this process of developing concepts to suit the resident capabilities may not deliver an optimised application of air power, even within the resource-availability balance that has to be maintained. There is an increasing need to take a different approach to establishing the relationship between concepts and capabilities. The evident volatility and unpredictability of the prevalent global security environment makes it necessary for a nation, and its air force, to develop strategic concepts as the first step to ensuring its security. It must then develop secondary concepts that will act as the blueprint for capability assessment. The capability requirement to satisfactorily embed these concepts in operations will come out of such an assessment. Only by doing so can a nation ensure its security with a believable probability of assurance.

Air power capabilities of the 'right' calibre are expensive; there is no denying this fact. Most democratic nations of the world, considering themselves to be in a state of peace, baulk at procuring cutting edge air power capabilities because of their resource-intensive nature. However, governments with a long-term view of national security—and also an understanding of the long lead-time required to field adequately sophisticated air power capabilities—will make informed decisions regarding resource allocation. These decisions will no doubt have far-reaching consequences for a nation's air power capabilities and also for the broader concept of national security. Therefore, they cannot be arrived at lightly and must be taken with the serious consideration that they deserve.

Considering the conflicting factors of high resource requirement and possibly constrained resource availability, it is easy to see that a national assessment of air power capability requirements vis-à-vis future national security needs will be a multifaceted process. The picture that emerges is not necessarily a rosy one. While the resource allocation debate is at a higher level of national security decisions, the challenges that these decisions will bring about will percolate down to the military strategic level, where they will have to be addressed. The situation tailor-made to create tensions, for primacy and relevance, between the agencies responsible for concept development and capability acquisition. Any contemporary air force that continues to develop its concepts to cater for available capability will be invariably on a retrograde path leading to 'non-success' and subsequent irrelevance. This holds true even for the immediate short-term, and obviously for the long-term.

Air forces that are, or aspire to be, of strategic relevance to a nation must already have adopted a concept-led capability development process or start the changeover immediately if they are to remain influential elements of national power in the future. Air power concepts must ensure national security and air power practitioners should be able to demonstrate to the government that the capabilities that can optimally employ the concepts are not negotiable requirements that can be diluted. This single factor forms an indelible part of ensuring the nation's security.

People

People have always been, and will continue to be, the bedrock on which successful application of air power is built. This will not change. However, the characteristics of the personnel required—in terms of education, attitude, aptitude, individual ethos, intangible qualities like leadership, integrity, and loyalty—who will be the best equipped to employ air power optimally will obviously evolve. The appropriate mix of qualities necessary is difficult to list or predict since the variables are far too many and a number of them are intangible. While the optimisation of personal characteristics in an airman is always a complex process, it is of the utmost importance to ensure that personnel with the appropriate mix of traits are carefully crafted as a team to employ air power effectively. Unfortunately the characteristics of an ideal airman—here the term airman is being used in a gender neutral manner and means a 'person' involved in the generation and application of air power—cannot be defined comprehensively since some of the traits are not clearly quantifiable.

Since technology makes air power capabilities continually evolving entities, the practice of the application of air power as a profession also has to keep pace. This demands keeping a constant watch on the skill base required of the work force to be efficient. A successful air force will be able to tailor the recruitment, training and education of its personnel in a flexible manner to meet an overarching strategic requirement of what is, and will be, expected of air power professionals, now and into the future.

Professional mastery of the force, the sum total of the professional mastery of the individual airmen who constitute the air force, will determine the future relevance of air power.[14] Creating a workforce with adequate numerical spread and with the necessary depth of professional mastery to cater for planned and random departures is an arduous and up-hill task. This cannot be achieved in a short period of time and requires long term planning and unwavering commitment. For an air force to reach a minimum level of acceptable competence, or to be elevate to this stature, professional airmen will have to work at their optimum, continually and without failure for a long time. Collective professionalism is equally important in maintaining an air force at the necessary level of competence at all times, indefinitely. This is the only way to ensure that the air force is capable of providing rapid and ready response to emerging security challenges that are likely to beset the nation. Like any other power projection capability, air power is also fallible. Only the professional mastery of airmen will reduce the probability of this fallibility to an acceptably low level and

---

14 For a more detailed examination of Professional Mastery, read Kainikara, Sanu, *Professional Mastery and Air Power Education*, Working Paper No 33, Air Power Development Centre, Canberra, October 2011.

elevate air power to its deserved status as the power element of first choice response in the national security calculus.

It is necessary for military leaders at all levels to be professional masters of their domains. In the case of air power, the dynamism inherent in its generation and application makes this a doubly critical requirement.[15] The necessary level of professional mastery of air power cannot be achieved overnight even with an intense dose of education, but is a process that has to be embedded within the culture and ethos of the force. Air forces that are numerically small will always face the challenge of balancing operational requirements with the need to embed an unbroken continuum of education for its cadres. This is a point of force development that should be a focal point for the senior leadership. Nurturing professional mastery cannot be given secondary status if the force is to remain strategically relevant in the long term. Professional mastery of its personnel is the cornerstone of the performance of an air force. In the current politico-economic situation, non-performance is an option that can be exercised by an air force only once. A government will be unwilling to carry a resource-intensive air force that does not deliver the needed effects when desired.

From a personnel perspective, the dynamism that has been alluded to in the previous paragraph is in the ability of the force as a whole understanding the changing needs of air power—in its generation, application and sustainment. Modern air power systems are extremely sophisticated and function at the very apex of the technology spectrum. Accordingly, it requires people with agile minds to fully understand the concepts being developed, the capabilities being fielded to put into operation those concepts and to fuse the two in a seamless manner into a cohesive whole that becomes the spear point of air power application aligned with national security imperatives. It is becoming increasingly apparent that the very same people will also have to determine the aim point for the spear so that national objectives are achieved. In the future, air power will be best served by people who are professional masters with highly developed skills and extremely agile minds.

---

15 Here it is not being suggested that military leaders in other domains do not have to be professional masters. This monograph is focused on air power and air forces and therefore added emphasis has been given to the requirements of air force leadership.

Organisation

The terms air force and force when used to denote the repository of national air power actually means the organisation that facilitates the coming together of concepts at the strategic and operational levels, capabilities that support the application of these concepts contextually, and people who are professional masters in the generation, application and sustainment of air power. An optimised organisation will, when all inputs are also equally optimised, deliver air power of a calibre that is able to sweep away all in its way. Continuing the analogy of the spear, organisation is the hand that holds the spear steady at the time of its employment—and like any weapon-holding and wielding hand, it has to be strong, supple and ambidextrous. In organisational terms these qualities translate to being robust, flexible and inherently agile.

A cursory examination of air forces that perform to the required standards easily reveal the fact that they are organisationally flexible. There are also sufficiently clear indications that the future will not be kind to air forces that become organisationally lethargic, irrespective of the brilliance of the concepts they develop and/or the capabilities they possess in support. Air power is considered by far the most dynamic of all power projection capabilities and success or failure in its application—translated to victory or defeat in the battlefield—is determined by the ability of the force to convert the dynamism of the organisation into forging a fighting force. The ability to do so is enhanced or worsened by the agility or lethargy of the organisational process that forges the force. In order to meet the contemporary demands of unpredictable security challenges an air force organisation must, of necessity, remain in a state of flux. The organisation must be able to perpetually adapt to the vagaries of the emerging security environment while continuing to be sufficiently robust in order to provide the necessary rigidity to create the framework that supports current and on-going operations. This is a complex demand.

Future organisations that control the intricate process of generation, application and sustainment of air power will have to be particularly agile. At the same time they must also be able to leave some areas of development open-ended in order to accept and accommodate the various, and at time unexpected, inputs that would be continually fed to the core of the organisational nervous system. The need to embrace this extreme dynamism will have to be tempered with an inherent robustness necessary to give the organisation its form and organisational agility. Further, dynamic agility would need to be trimmed with sufficient rigidity in the structure to ensure that on-going operations are adequately supported. To achieve an organisation with these somewhat conflicting characteristics, the dynamism will have to be kept evolutionary, while the robustness should be induced with a certain amount of built-in flexibility to provide a suppleness to its rigidity. An organisation's acceptance level of dynamic inputs will be dependent on the balance that is maintained between these two opposing but fundamental requirements.

Conclusion

The focal points that have been discussed are just that—focal points. An air force that does not continually and constantly monitor these focal points and initiate remedial action as soon as a discrepancy is noticed will be sliding down a road to failure. It is the organisation, an amorphous entity made up of people and ideas that makes a tangible connection between air power and national security imperatives. The focal points that have been discussed in this chapter are all-encompassing and combine the pragmatic and the intangible; the known and the emerging unknown; entrenched capabilities and sophisticated concepts.

Like everything else in the realm of air power, there will always be an overarching sense of change in all aspects of the focal points, and it should rightly be so. From an air force perspective, staying static in any aspect is indeed a recipe for failure. The professional mastery of airmen in itself is a dynamic quality that cannot be assumed to be automatically present because the force had displayed it previously. Maintaining the necessary level of professional mastery, individually and the force as a whole, is also a continual process that is neglected at the peril of the force declining in its overall capability. In the future, as is apparent even now, only an air force that keeps the four focal points at an adequate level of competence, which itself will vary contextually and in the medium term, can hope to deliver the necessary quantity of quality air power as and when the nation demands it.

CONCLUSION

'At first novel, then startling, and now phenomenal, the rise of air power has erected many crucial problems for statesmen and strategists. It has become the most powerful force underwriting the policy of nations in their relations with one another.'

Eugene M. Emme[16]

The future is filled with questions and while they are being addressed there is no way to assure that the answers that are forthcoming are the correct ones. The list of challenges that air power faces is long, especially at the operational level. Most of them have been part of the developmental scenario of air power, manifesting in different ways at different times in the evolution of this critical military capability. It is necessary to understand them since they are fundamental to future developments and will continue to stare at air power professionals almost continually at all times. There is also a sense of urgency in providing the answers and solutions to emerging challenges to national security that add to the complexity of addressing them. Often, air power comes into this equation without sufficient preparation and therefore is perceived to have performed at a less than optimal fashion. Even so it is necessary to question future possibilities in order to understand the current path that air power is following and to reflect on the possible future capabilities.

The day that air power capabilities resident in a nation's air force becomes misaligned with, and/or unresponsive to, the national demands of contemporary security requirements, will be the day that the force starts on a downward path, which can rapidly develop into an unrecoverable death spiral. Air power has to continually and consciously adapt to new

---

16 Emme, Eugene M. *op cit*, p. 18.

and emerging paradigms. Air power and air forces have been adept at focusing on the future and in adapting to incessant changes in the security environment and accommodating evolving capabilities, most of the time in an evolutionary manner. The resilience of an air force is directly dependent on the rate at which the force is capable of adapting to change, which in turn is in direct proportion to the flexibility—both doctrinal and operational—inherent in the force. This is not a capacity that can be built overnight and once embedded in a force through concerted training and education requires careful nurturing at all times.

Air power embeds all the capabilities and competencies necessary to perform its assigned tasks. The need of the hour is to conceptualise the way in which these capabilities can be optimally employed to meet the ultimate national security imperatives. At the very moment that air power strategists believe that they have met all the demands that could conceivably be placed on air power, new challenges and issues almost always crop up.

The future will never be what it is predicted to be, it will always spring surprises—irrespective of the veracity of the crystal ball in use.

There is an issue that air power continually faces and which has only been alluded to in the chapters of the book—why is the control and employment of air power so contentious? Why is it that the other Services always demand that they control air power through the command of its assets, while tenaciously holding on to the command and control of their own domain-centric assets? Although the issue was somewhat ameliorated in the aftermath of World War II, it has raised its hackles again in the past decade or so. The great potential of air power in terms of its capabilities and employment options, both in peace and war, is the fundamental reason for this unwarranted power grab. There is no doubt that air power is the foremost capability that comprehensively supports all the principles of war, but its efficacy is determined by the professional mastery of airmen. The application of air power in a flexible and cohesive manner cannot be achieved by anyone else, but professionals who are steeped in the history, strategy and application of air power—a lifelong study if ever there was one. However, watch out for the impending scramble for control of air power vis-à-vis the national security strategy.

Conclusion

As the global society continues to evolve, the questions and debate regarding the morality of applying lethal force is becoming more vociferous and increasingly frequent. This is particularly pronounced when applied to the actions of sovereign nation-states. The onus of responsibility to ensure that the moral, legal and ethical requirements in the application of lethal force are met will fall to the 'warriors', the practitioners of the art of war, who would now not only have to lead the armed forces in conflict and war, but also have to become statesmen of calibre. They will be the arbiters for the optimised employment of force while ensuring that the nation is always placed on the right side of morality—always functioning from the much vaunted moral high ground.

If a nation-state is to continue to ensure its sovereignty in the clearly murky future that is emerging, the ability to apply lethal force at the time and place of its choosing will remain an unfortunate but necessary capability. The complexities of applying this capability points to the fact that in the future it will be necessary to have an overlap, rather than an interaction, in the national leadership between the military and the grand strategic level of decision-making.

The probability of a full-fledged state-on-state conflict erupting in the near future is very low. On the other hand there is high chances of instability and accompanying geo-strategic volatility breaking out in some regions. These occurrences will invariably lead to asymmetric, irregular conflicts that has gradually become the norm. The need to stabilise these regions have led to the formation of international coalitions, with or without the sanction of the United Nations. While flexible response options to stabilisation demands full spectrum military capabilities, all military forces do not possess such capabilities. However, even smaller nations find it necessary to contribute to stabilisation operations.

The compulsion for small nations to contribute to stabilisation operations that could lead to IW could stem from two fundamental reasons. One is the need to stay relevant in the international political environment or the global commons; and two, to ensure that their own security is ensured through pleasing a powerful 'friend'. Whether the campaign is purely for stabilisation, peace-keeping or even peace-enforcement, the conventional forces will require control of the air.

Smaller nations as coalition partners will find it difficult to deploy adequate air power capabilities, even if it is 'niche'. The situation is perilous for smaller nations—air power or the lack of it could lead them down the path of irrelevance.

The status of national air power capabilities resident in the air force, especially of a small or medium power nation, is directly dependent on its international political status. The air force also needs to have a minimum level of technology acceptance to be able to function at the bare minimum level of efficiency. Going below either of these levels, will be the air force entering a death-spiral. While it is possible to pull out of such a situation, the time to come back to the previous level will be double of what it took to become irrelevant. The force will struggle to become combative and efficient again. Technology acceptance itself is a critical capability. The nurturing of this capability is a political decision at the national level and the air force has only peripheral influence in ensuring its adequacy.

Another aspect of political influence as air power explores new avenues of exploitation is the fact that it will be forced to operate within increasingly restrictive rules of engagement. For a variety of reasons, the democratic nations of the world, who are doing the bulk of stabilisation duties, will continue to place further restriction on the use of lethal force especially when employed for the air. Air Force will have to comply. The result will be that air power will be reliant almost entirely on its flexibility to be effective, while also forfeiting some of its agility. The balance will depend on the strategic command ability of the force leadership. Strategic leadership will be critical to the future effectiveness of air power and air forces.

The technology-dependence of air power will continue to increase. Middle power nations will be hard pressed to find an optimum balance between domestic political expediency and resource allocation. The balance will determine the future efficacy of the air force. The best method to maintain the correct balance would be to examine the resource allocation quandary through the prism of a cost-benefit analysis. Any other methodology will find air power coming out the loser. In this monograph, space-dependence of air power has only been superficially touched upon. This is so since middle power nations are almost totally dependent on political alliances to provide the necessary

Conclusion

space capabilities for their air forces. There are only a handful of nations in the world who can claim independent space-capability. In the broader analysis of the future of air power, space therefore takes a unilaterally political position.

The legal, moral and ethical debate regarding the employment of UAVs and UCAVs is unlikely to be resolved in the near future. At the risk of being politically incorrect the author would like to point out that the most vociferous critics of the use of UCAVs are the irregular entities, and nations that support them, who do not possess these capabilities. It is proposed here that UCAVs are the asymmetry of conventional national forces and should be considered a counter to the suicide bombings that terrorists resort to when faced with overwhelming military force.

Contemporary air power is brimming with a sense of urgent change; of being at the edge of momentous developments. The future sky is tangibly 'blue'.

'I know not with what weapons World War III will be fought, but World War IV will be fought with sticks and stones.'

—**Albert Einstein**

'Sixteen hours ago an American airplane dropped one bomb on Hiroshima . . . The force from which the sun draws its power has been loosed against those who brought war to the Far East.'

First announcement of the atomic bomb, August 6, 1945

—**Harry S Truman,** Then President of the USA

SELECTED BIBLIOGRAPHY

Budiansky, Stephen, *Air Power*, Penguin Books, London, 2003.

Creveld, Martin van, *The Age of Air Power*, Public Affairs, New York, 2011.

Emme, Eugene M., (ed), *The Impact of Air Power: National Security and World Politics*, D. Van Nostrand Company Inc., Princeton, New Jersey, 1959.

Farley, Robert M., *Grounded: The Case for Abolishing the United States Air Force*, University Press of Kentucky, Kentucky, 2014.

Gray, Peter W (ed), *Air Power 21: Challenges for the New Century*, The Stationary Office, London, 2000.

Hallion, Dr Richard P. (ed), *Air Power Confronts an Unstable World*, Brassey's UK (Ltd), 1997.

Hayward, Joel (ed), *Air Power, Insurgency and the "War on Terror"*, RAF Centre for Air Power Studies, Cranwell, UK, 2009.

Kainikara, Sanu, *The Art of Air Power: Sun Tzu Revisted*, Air Power Development Centre, Canberra, 2009.

Olsen, John Andreas (ed), *Air Power Reborn*, Naval Institute Press, Annapolis, Maryland, 2015.

Pearson, Simon, *Total War 2006*, Hodder and Stoughton, London, 1999.

Pillsbury, Michael (ed), *Chinese Views on Future Warfare*, Lancer Publishers, New Delhi, 1997.

Singer, P.W., *Wired for War*, The Penguin Press, New York, 2009.

Vick, Alan; Stillion David R., and others, *Aerospace Operations in Urban Environments: Exploring New Concepts*, RAND, Santa Monica, CA, 2000.

Index

A

Aerospace technology 41

Air Power iii, vi, ix, xii, xiii, xxiv, xxx, 1, 9, 17, 35, 40, 75, 82, 93

Arnold, General Henry H. 75

Artificial intelligence (AI) xxix, 49, 50, 58, 64, 65, 66, 67, 68, 69, 70, 71, 72

B

Battlespace xiv, xvi, 11, 12, 49, 50, 51, 52, 69, 70, 71

C

Cassandra i, iii, vii, xxvi

Chun, Clayton K.S. 57

Classifying Wars

    wars of choice 3

    wars of necessity 3

Coalition Operations 30

Cold War 4

Collateral Damage 24

D

Directed energy (DE) 50

Dugan, General Mike xix

E

Electronic warfare (EW) 50

F

Factors to effectively employ cutting edge technology

    level of technology-acceptance 36

    national education base 36

First choice Response Option 21

H

High-end technology 36

High-latitude, long-endurance (HALE) 59

Humanitarian aid and disaster relief (HADR) xxii, 73

I

Improvised explosive devices 59, 73

Intelligence, surveillance and reconnaissance (ISR)   xvi, xxvi, xxix, 10, 12, 13, 51, 59, 60, 62, 70, 72

Irregular Warfare   5

Irregular wars (IW)   xxv, xxvii, 5, 7, 8, 9, 11, 12, 13, 14, 15, 16, 27, 29, 45, 46, 89

K

King Priam   vii

Kosovo   xix, 2

Kunduz   26

L

Laws of Armed Conflict (LOAC)   24, 25, 32, 62

Libya   xiii, 79

M

Man-portable air defence systems (MANPADS)   63

Marshal, George C.   1

Martin van Creveld   xii

Mujahedeen   63

N

National Education Base   36

National Security   xxii, 1, 75, 93

NATO   xiii, 2, 79

O

Olsen, John Andreas   17

OODA loop   49

Operation Unified Protector   xiii, 79

Q

Queen Hecuba   vii

R

Rosier, Sir Fredrick   35

S

Smith, Rupert   19

Soviet Union   4

U

Uninhabited Aerial Systems (UAS)   72, 73

Uninhabited aerial vehicles (UAVs)   xxix, 57, 58, 59, 60, 64, 68, 70, 71, 72, 73, 91

Uninhabited combat aerial vehicles (UCAVs)   xxix, 58, 59, 60, 61, 62, 63, 64, 65, 67, 68, 69, 70, 71, 72, 73, 91

V

Vallance, Air Commodore G B   xxx

W

Wars of national survival   4

World War II   2, 7, 43, 44, 77, 88

www.ingramcontent.com/pod-product-compliance
Lightning Source LLC
Chambersburg PA
CBHW022142160426
43197CB00009B/1390